BUDGET-FRIENDLY
DIABETIC
⟨ FOOD ⟩
ENCYCLOPEDIA

The Explosive Low-GI Food Guide to Master Pre-Diabetes,
Type 1 & 2 Diabetes with Ease.
Includes a No-Fuss Beginner's Cookbook with Low-Carb
and Low-Sugar Tasty Recipes

ROSY LUKE

Copyright © 2024 by Rosy Luke
Diabetic Food Encyclopedia

ISBN: 979-8885077712
10 9 8 7 6 5 4 3 2 1
All Right Reserved

GET YOUR EXTRA CONTENT NOW!

To download the digital version of these bonuses you don't need to enter any details except your name and email address.

EXTRA#1
Blood Sugar Log Book

EXTRA#2
Food Journal Log Book

EXTRA#3
Medication Log Book

EXTRA#4
Recipe Remix: Adapting Favorites for Diabetic Health

EXTRA#5
Dine Out Smart: A Diabetic's Guide to Eating Out

SIMPLY SCAN THE QR CODE BELOW OR GO TO

bonusbooklovers.com/rosy-luke-de

Table of Contents

CHAPTER 1: INTRODUCTION TO DIABETES AND NUTRITION 7
- UNDERSTANDING DIABETES 8
- ROLE OF DIET 9

CHAPTER 2: CARBOHYDRATES IN DEPTH 11
- UNDERSTANDING CARBS 11
- CARB-COUNTING 12

CHAPTER 3: PROTEINS 15
- TYPES OF PROTEIN 15

CHAPTER 4: FATS 17
- IDENTIFYING HEALTHY FATS 17
- AVOIDING UNHEALTHY FATS 18

CHAPTER 5: FIBER'S ROLE IN DIABETES CONTROL 20
- HIGH-FIBER FOODS 20

CHAPTER 6: VITAMINS AND MINERALS ESSENTIAL FOR DIABETICS 24
- KEY NUTRIENTS 24
- NUTRIENT-DENSE FOODS 25

CHAPTER 7: GLYCEMIC INDEX AND DIABETES 27
- GLYCEMIC INDEX EXPLAINED 27
- LOW GLYCEMIC CHOICES 28

CHAPTER 8: COMPREHENSIVE FOOD LISTS FOR DIABETICS 30
- BEANS 30
- DARK GREEN LEAFY VEGETABLES 34
- CITRUS FRUITS 38
- BERRIES 43
- TOMATOES 45

CHAPTER 9: FISH HIGH IN OMEGA-3 FATTY ACIDS 48
- SALMON 48
- HERRING 49
- SARDINES 50

CHAPTER 10: ADVANCED DIABETIC MENU PLANNING 52
- MEAL PLANNING 52

CHAPTER 11: BUSTING MYTHS ABOUT DIABETIC DIETS 54
- FACT-BASED INFORMATION 55

CHAPTER 12: ADDITIONAL RESOURCES 57
- READING LIST 57
- SUPPORT NETWORKS 58

CHAPTER 13: NAVIGATING FOOD LABELS .. 60
- DECODING NUTRITIONAL INFORMATION 60
- IDENTIFYING HIDDEN SUGARS 62
- UNDERSTANDING HEALTH CLAIMS 63
- MAKING SMART CHOICES 64
- INTERACTIVE EXAMPLES 65

CHAPTER 14: DIABETIC DIET BREAKFAST .. 68
- 1. GRILLED CHICKEN CAESAR SALAD 68
- 2. SPINACH AND FETA OMELETTE 68
- 3. GREEK YOGURT PARFAIT 69
- 4. AVOCADO TOAST 69
- 5. BERRY SMOOTHIE 70
- 6. VEGGIE BREAKFAST BURRITO 70
- 7. OVERNIGHT CHIA PUDDING 71
- 8. PEANUT BUTTER BANANA WRAP 71
- 9. QUINOA BREAKFAST BOWL 72
- 10. EGG AND VEGETABLE MUFFIN CUPS 72

CHAPTER 15: DIABETIC DIET LUNCH 73
- 11. GRILLED CHICKEN SALAD 73
- 12. QUINOA STUFFED BELL PEPPERS 73
- 13. SPINACH AND FETA OMELETTE 74

14. Tuna and Avocado Wrap 74
15. Caprese Pasta Salad 75
16. Chickpea and Vegetable Stir-Fry 75
17. Turkey and Hummus Wrap 76
18. Greek Yogurt and Berry Parfait 76
19. Shrimp Stir-Fry with Vegetables 77
20. Veggie Pita Pocket 77

CHAPTER 16: NO-FUSS RECIPES 78

21. Scrambled Egg and Vegetable Wrap 78
22. Greek Yogurt Parfait 78
23. Vegetable Omelette 79
24. Overnight Chia Pudding 79
25. Avocado Toast 80
26. Quinoa Breakfast Bowl 80
27. Veggie Breakfast Burrito 81
28. Spinach and Feta Quiche Cups 81
29. Berry Smoothie Bowl 82
30. Cottage Cheese and Fruit Salad 82
31. Chicken and Vegetable Stir-Fry 83
32. Quinoa Salad 83
33. Turkey Lettuce Wraps 84
34. Spinach and Mushroom Omelette 84
35. Salmon and Asparagus Foil Pack 85
36. Lentil Soup 85
37. Greek Salad with Grilled Chicken 86
38. Veggie and Hummus Wrap 86
39. Tofu and Vegetable Stir-Fry 87
40. Caprese Salad 87
41. Grilled Lemon Herb Chicken 88
42. Baked Salmon with Roasted Vegetables 88
43. Quinoa Stuffed Bell Peppers 89
44. Turkey and Vegetable Stir-Fry 89
45. Veggie and Tofu Curry 90
46. Shrimp and Broccoli Stir-Fry 90
47. Baked Chicken Parmesan 91
48. Lentil and Vegetable Soup 91
49. Baked Cod with Lemon and Herbs 92
50. Vegetable and Chickpea Curry 92
51. Apple Cinnamon Energy Bites 93
52. Chickpea Salad 93
53. Veggie Stuffed Mini Peppers 94

54. Avocado Hummus 94
55. Quinoa Salad Cups 95
56. Zucchini Chips 95
57. Tuna Lettuce Wraps 96
58. Baked Sweet Potato Fries 96
59. Berry Chia Pudding 97
60. Cucumber Mint Water 97
61. Apple Cinnamon Crumble 98
62. Chocolate Avocado Mousse 98
63. Banana Oatmeal Cookies 99
64. Lemon Yogurt Parfait 99
65. Peanut Butter Banana Ice Cream 100
66. Quinoa Fruit Salad 100
67. Baked Peaches with Honey and Cinnamon ... 101
68. Vanilla Chia Seed Pudding 101
69. Oatmeal Raisin Energy Balls 102
70. Strawberry Banana Smoothie 102

CHAPTER 17: 15-MINUTE RECIPES 103

71. Scrambled Egg and Avocado Wrap 103
72. Greek Yogurt Parfait 103
73. Spinach and Feta Omelette 104
74. Overnight Chia Pudding 104
75. Whole Wheat Banana Pancakes 105
76. Veggie and Cheese Breakfast Quesadilla 105
77. Berry and Spinach Smoothie 106
78. Smoked Salmon and Cream Cheese Bagel ... 106
79. Avocado and Tomato Toast 107
80. Fruit and Nut Breakfast Quinoa 107
81. Grilled Chicken Caesar Salad 108
82. Quinoa and Vegetable Stir-Fry 108
83. Turkey and Avocado Wrap 109
84. Caprese Pasta Salad 109
85. Salmon and Asparagus Foil Pack 110
86. Greek Chicken Pita 110
87. Egg Salad Lettuce Wraps 111
88. Veggie and Hummus Wrap 111
89. Tuna and White Bean Salad 112
90. Veggie Omelette 112
91. Grilled Salmon with Lemon and Dill 113
92. Grilled Chicken with Balsamic Glaze 113
93. Shrimp Stir-Fry with Vegetables 114

94. Beef and Broccoli Stir-Fry 114
95. Mediterranean Tuna Salad 115
96. Veggie Omelette 115
97. Quinoa Salad with Roasted Vegetables 116
98. Caprese Stuffed Chicken Breast 116
99. Spinach and Mushroom Frittata 117
100. Black Bean and Corn Salad 117
101. Avocado and Tomato Salad 118
102. Greek Yogurt with Berries 118
103. Veggie Wrap 119
104. Tuna Salad Lettuce Wraps 119
105. Caprese Skewers 120
106. Apple and Almond Butter Slices 120
107. Cucumber and Cream Cheese Bites 121
108. Edamame Salad 121
109. Roasted Chickpeas 122
110. Berry Smoothie 122
111. Chocolate Banana Pudding 123
112. Strawberry Yogurt Parfait 123
113. Apple Cinnamon Mug Cake 124
114. Chia Pudding with Berries 124
115. Peanut Butter Energy Balls 125
116. Greek Yogurt with Honey and Walnuts 125
117. Raspberry Chia Jam 126
118. Mango Coconut Chia Popsicles 126
119. Almond Flour Blueberry Muffins 127
120. Watermelon Fruit Pizza 127

CHAPTER 18: RECIPES ON A BUDGET 128

121. Scrambled Eggs with Vegetables 128
122. Oatmeal with Berries and Nuts 128
123. Greek Yogurt Parfait 129
124. Whole Wheat Pancakes 129
125. Vegetable Omelette 130
126. Avocado Toast with Egg 130
127. Cottage Cheese and Fruit Bowl 131
128. Breakfast Burrito 131
129. Fruit and Yogurt Smoothie 132
130. Veggie Breakfast Wrap 132
131. Chicken and Vegetable Stir-Fry 133
132. Turkey and Avocado Wrap 133

133. Tuna Salad Lettuce Wraps 134
134. Lentil and Vegetable Soup 134
135. Quinoa and Vegetable Salad 135
136. Spinach and Mushroom Omelette 135
137. Black Bean and Vegetable Quesadilla 136
138. Greek Salad with Grilled Chicken 136
139. Salmon and Asparagus Foil Packets 137
140. Veggie and Hummus Wrap 137
141. Grilled Lemon Herb Chicken Breast 138
142. Baked Salmon with Dill Sauce 138
143. Turkey and Vegetable Stir-Fry 139
144. Quinoa and Black Bean Salad 139
145. Vegetable Curry with Brown Rice 140
146. Spinach and Feta Stuffed Chicken Breast.. 140
147. Lentil and Vegetable Soup 141
148. Shrimp and Broccoli Stir-Fry 141
149. Eggplant Parmesan 142
150. Greek Salad with Grilled Chicken 142
151. Roasted Chickpeas 143
152. Greek Yogurt Parfait 143
153. Veggie Sticks with Hummus 144
154. Baked Sweet Potato Chips 144
155. Tuna Salad Lettuce Wraps 145
156. Apple Slices with Peanut Butter 145
157. Cottage Cheese and Berries 146
158. Mini Caprese Skewers 146
159. Hard-Boiled Eggs with Salt and Pepper 147
160. Rice Cake with Avocado and Tomato 147
161. Easy Berry Parfait 148
162. Chocolate Avocado Mousse 148
163. Apple Cinnamon Oatmeal Cookies 149
164. Banana Ice Cream 149
165. Lemon Chia Seed Pudding 150
166. Peanut Butter Energy Balls 150
167. Vanilla Chia Pudding 151
168. Baked Cinnamon Apple Chips 151
169. Pumpkin Spice Muffins 152
170. Greek Yogurt Bark 152

CHAPTER 19: CONVERSION CHART 153

INDEX 156

CHAPTER 1: INTRODUCTION TO DIABETES AND NUTRITION

Diabetes is a chronic medical condition that affects millions of people worldwide. It is characterized by high levels of glucose in the blood, either due to the body's inability to produce enough insulin or the inability to use insulin effectively. This condition can lead to various health complications if not properly managed. Nutrition is an important aspect of diabetes management since it helps to control blood sugar levels and preserve general health. There are several types of diabetes, each with its own unique characteristics. The most common types include type 1 diabetes, type 2 diabetes, and gestational diabetes. Type 1 diabetes is an autoimmune illness in which the immune system erroneously assaults and kills insulin-producing cells in the pancreas. Type 1 diabetics require insulin injections to keep their blood sugar levels under control. Type 2 diabetes, on the other hand, is a metabolic illness defined by insulin resistance, which occurs when the cells in the body do not respond effectively to insulin. This kind of diabetes is frequently linked to lifestyle choices such as poor food, lack of physical activity, and obesity.

Gestational diabetes develops during pregnancy and often cures after childbirth, but it raises the chance of acquiring type 2 diabetes later in life.

Common diabetes symptoms include frequent urination, excessive thirst, unexplained weight loss, increased appetite, exhaustion, and impaired eyesight. Diabetes, if left untreated, can cause major consequences such as heart disease, stroke, kidney disease, nerve damage, and vision issues. Therefore, it is crucial for individuals with diabetes to manage their condition effectively through lifestyle modifications, including a healthy diet.

Diabetes control requires careful attention to diet. The food we eat directly influences our blood sugar levels, thus it is important to make informed decisions about what we consume. A well-balanced and healthy diet can help manage blood sugar levels, enhance insulin sensitivity, and reduce the risk of diabetic complications. The key principles of a healthy diabetes diet include consuming a variety of foods from different food groups, controlling portion sizes, monitoring carbohydrate intake, and limiting the consumption of sugary and processed foods.

Incorporating whole grains, lean proteins, fruits, vegetables, and healthy fats into one's diet is highly recommended for individuals with diabetes. These foods provide essential nutrients, vitamins, and minerals while helping to maintain stable blood sugar levels. It is also important to be mindful of the glycemic index (GI) of foods, which measures how quickly a particular food raises blood sugar levels. Foods with a low GI are preferable, as they have a slower and more gradual impact on blood sugar.

In addition to making healthy food choices, regular physical activity is also crucial for managing diabetes. Exercise helps improve insulin sensitivity, promotes weight loss, and reduces the risk of cardiovascular complications. It is advised to do at least 150 minutes of moderate-intensity aerobic activity every week, as well as strength training activities.

Understanding Diabetes

Diabetes is a complex and chronic condition that affects millions of people worldwide. In order to gain a comprehensive understanding of this disease, it is important to explore the differences between the three main types: Type 1 diabetes, Type 2 diabetes, and gestational diabetes. By delving into the causes and impacts of each type, we can shed light on the intricacies of this condition and the importance of managing it effectively.

Type 1 diabetes, also known as insulin-dependent diabetes, is an autoimmune disease that typically develops in childhood or adolescence. In this kind of diabetes, the immune system incorrectly assaults and kills insulin-producing cells in the pancreas. As a result, the body is unable to produce enough insulin, a hormone essential for regulating blood sugar levels. Without enough insulin, glucose accumulates in the circulation, resulting in elevated blood sugar levels. Individuals with Type 1 diabetes need lifelong insulin treatment to survive.

Type 2 diabetes, on the other hand, is characterized by insulin resistance and insufficient insulin production. This kind of diabetes is frequently related with lifestyle factors such as poor nutrition, sedentary activity, and obesity. Over time, the body's cells become less responsive to insulin, and the pancreas struggles to keep up with the demand for insulin production. As a result, blood sugar levels rise, leading to the development of Type 2 diabetes. While this kind of diabetes is more frequent in adults, it is also being diagnosed in children and adolescents as obesity rates rise. Gestational diabetes develops during pregnancy and affects between 2 and 10% of pregnant moms. It is caused by hormonal changes that make the body less responsive to insulin, resulting in high blood sugar levels. Most women with gestational diabetes do not experience any symptoms, which is why it is crucial for pregnant women to undergo routine screenings. If left untreated, gestational diabetes can lead to complications for both the mother and the baby. However, with proper management and monitoring, most women are able to control their blood sugar levels and have a healthy pregnancy.

While understanding the differences between these three types of diabetes is important, it is equally crucial to recognize the common impacts they can have on individuals' health. High blood sugar levels, if left uncontrolled, can lead to a range of complications. These may include cardiovascular disease, kidney damage, nerve damage, vision problems, and an increased risk of infections. It is therefore imperative for individuals with diabetes to actively manage their condition and maintain good blood sugar control.

Diabetes management requires a complex strategy that includes frequent blood sugar testing, a nutritious diet, regular physical exercise, and, in some circumstances, medication or insulin therapy. By adopting a balanced and nutritious diet, individuals can help regulate their blood sugar levels and maintain a healthy weight. Regular exercise not only increases insulin sensitivity but also promotes general health. Additionally, medication and insulin therapy may be prescribed to help manage blood sugar levels effectively.

By adopting a proactive approach to managing diabetes, individuals can minimize the risk of complications and lead a fulfilling life. It is important to raise awareness about this condition and promote education to empower individuals to make informed decisions regarding their health.

Role of Diet

The role of diet in managing diabetes is of utmost importance when it comes to controlling blood glucose levels and preventing complications. A well-balanced diet, portion control, and careful food choices are essential components of a successful dietary management plan for individuals living with diabetes.

Portion control is another key aspect of managing diabetes through diet. It involves being mindful of the quantity of food consumed at each meal and snack. Individuals who restrict their portion sizes can better manage their blood sugar levels and avoid glucose spikes or decreases. This may be accomplished by using smaller plates, measuring meal quantities, and being mindful of the serving sizes suggested by healthcare specialists.

In addition to balanced meals and portion control, understanding the types of foods to consume and avoid is crucial for effective dietary management. Foods that are high in added sugars, unhealthy fats, and refined carbohydrates should be limited or avoided, as they can cause blood sugar levels to rise rapidly. Instead, individuals should focus on consuming whole foods such as fruits, vegetables, whole grains, lean proteins, and healthy fats. These foods have a lower glycemic index, which means they have a slower and more gradual impact on blood sugar levels.

Meal planning is a valuable tool in diabetes management. Planning meals in advance allows individuals to make healthier food choices, control portion sizes, and maintain consistent meal timings. It also helps prevent impulsive food decisions and reduces the likelihood of consuming foods that may negatively affect blood glucose levels. When planning meals, individuals should aim to include a variety of foods from different food groups and consider the carbohydrate content of each meal to ensure a balanced intake.

Regular meal timings are essential for individuals with diabetes. Eating at regular intervals throughout the day helps to maintain blood sugar levels and avoid excessive variations. Skipping meals or going long periods without eating can lead to unstable glucose levels and potential complications. It is recommended to have three main meals and two to three small snacks evenly spaced throughout the day.

While the importance of a balanced diet, portion control, meal planning, and regular meal timings are well-established in managing diabetes, it is important to note that incorporating specific recipes and exercises into the dietary management plan can further enhance its effectiveness. Recipes that focus on whole, unprocessed ingredients and are low in added sugars and unhealthy fats can help individuals with diabetes maintain a healthy diet while enjoying flavorful meals. Regular physical exercise is also important in diabetes care because it improves insulin sensitivity, helps regulate weight, and lowers blood sugar. Engaging in activities such as walking, swimming, cycling, or strength training can be beneficial for individuals with diabetes.

By adopting a comprehensive approach to dietary management, individuals can lead healthier lives and reduce the risk of diabetes-related complications.

CHAPTER 2: CARBOHYDRATES IN DEPTH

Carbohydrates are one of the three macronutrients, along with fats and proteins. They are the body's primary source of energy and are present in a wide range of foods such as cereals, fruits, vegetables, dairy products, and sweets. When carbs are ingested, they are converted into glucose, which the body subsequently uses for energy.

There are three forms of carbohydrates: sugars, starches, and fiber. Sugars are simple carbohydrates that are easily taken into the circulation, causing a fast rise in blood glucose levels. Starches, on the other hand, are complex carbohydrates that take longer to digest and have a more gradual impact on blood sugar. Fiber, although technically a carbohydrate, is not digested by the body and does not raise blood sugar levels.

For individuals with diabetes, it is important to monitor carbohydrate intake and choose carbohydrates that have a minimal impact on blood sugar. This can be done by understanding the glycemic index (GI) of different foods. As previously stated, the GI assesses how rapidly a carbohydrate-rich diet elevates blood sugar levels. Foods with a high GI, such as white bread and sugary drinks, cause a rapid increase in blood sugar, while foods with a low GI, such as whole grains and non-starchy vegetables, have a slower and more controlled effect.

In addition to the GI, portion control is also crucial for managing blood sugar levels, which has been previously touched upon. Even low-GI meals can induce a surge in blood sugar if ingested in big quantities. Therefore, it is important to balance carbohydrate intake with other macronutrients and to spread out carbohydrate consumption throughout the day.

Furthermore, the timing of carbohydrate consumption can also affect blood sugar levels. Eating carbohydrates in combination with protein and healthy fats can help slow down the digestion and absorption of carbohydrates, resulting in a more gradual increase in blood sugar.

Understanding Carbs

Carbohydrates provide us with energy, fueling our daily activities and bodily functions. However, not all carbohydrates are created equal. There are two main types of carbs: simple and complex. Understanding the difference between these two types is crucial, as it directly impacts our blood sugar levels and overall health.

Simple carbohydrates, also known as simple sugars, are composed of one or two sugar molecules. They are quickly digested and absorbed by the body, leading to a rapid increase in blood sugar levels.

This abrupt rise in blood sugar gives you a burst of energy, but it's short-lived and usually followed by a collapse. Sugary beverages, candy, pastries, and white bread are all high in simple carbohydrates.

On the other hand, complex carbohydrates are made up of longer chains of sugar molecules. These chains take longer to degrade and are more slowly absorbed by the body. As a result, complex carbs have a gentler impact on blood sugar levels, providing a steady release of energy over a longer period. Examples of foods rich in complex carbs include whole grains, legumes, vegetables, and fruits.

The glycemic index (GI) is a measure that ranks carbohydrates based on their effect on blood sugar levels. Foods with a high glycemic index cause blood sugar levels to rise quickly, whereas foods with a low glycemic index produce a more gradual rise. It is important to note that not all simple carbs have a high GI, and not all complex carbs have a low GI. Factors such as processing, cooking methods, and the presence of fiber can influence the glycemic index of a food.

Balancing carbohydrates with other nutrients is crucial for maintaining stable blood sugar levels and overall health. Including protein and healthy fats in meals can help decrease carb digestion and absorption, reducing blood sugar increases. For example, combining a piece of fruit with a handful of almonds or incorporating lean protein into a whole grain dish can result in a more balanced and fulfilling dinner.

To better understand the impact of simple and complex carbohydrates on blood sugar levels, let's consider an example. Imagine eating a candy bar made with simple carbs. Within minutes, the sugar from the candy bar enters your bloodstream, causing a rapid increase in blood sugar levels. This sudden surge triggers the release of insulin, a hormone that helps regulate blood sugar. However, the insulin response may be too strong, leading to a rapid drop in blood sugar levels, leaving you feeling tired and craving more sugar.

On the other hand, if you were to have a meal consisting of complex carbohydrates, such as whole grain pasta with vegetables and lean protein, the digestion and absorption process would be slower. This gradual release of sugar into the bloodstream allows for a more balanced and sustained energy release. As a result, you feel satisfied for a longer period and experience fewer cravings.

By choosing complex carbs over simple carbs and balancing them with other nutrients, we can maintain stable energy levels, support weight management, and reduce the risk of chronic diseases. So, next time you reach for a snack or plan a meal, remember the power of carbs and make informed choices for your well-being.

Carb-Counting

Maintaining balanced blood sugar levels is crucial for individuals with diabetes, and one effective method to achieve this is through carbohydrate counting. This comprehensive guide, titled "B. Carb-

Counting," aims to provide a detailed explanation of carbohydrate counting, its significance in managing diabetes, and practical strategies for incorporating it into daily life. By understanding the different types of carbohydrates, the glycemic index, the importance of combining carbs with proteins and healthy fats, and the role of portion control, individuals can gain better control over their blood sugar levels. Furthermore, this guide offers practical exercises and delicious recipes to help individuals apply their newfound knowledge in a meaningful way.

Understanding Carbohydrates

Carbohydrates are a vital source of energy for the body, but not all carbs are created equal. This section explores the different types of carbohydrates, including simple and complex carbs, and their impact on blood sugar levels. By understanding the glycemic index, individuals can make informed choices about the carbohydrates they consume, promoting better blood sugar management.

Section 2: The Significance of Combining Carbs with Proteins and Healthy Fats

While carbohydrates are essential, combining them with proteins and healthy fats can help regulate blood sugar levels more effectively. This section delves into the importance of balanced meals and snacks that incorporate all three macronutrients. By understanding how proteins and healthy fats slow down the digestion of carbohydrates, individuals can prevent blood sugar spikes and maintain stable levels throughout the day.

Portion Control: The Key to Balanced Carbohydrate Intake

Portion control plays a pivotal role in carbohydrate counting. This section provides practical tips and techniques for estimating portion sizes and monitoring carbohydrate intake. By learning how to measure and visualize appropriate portions, individuals can better manage their blood sugar levels and make informed choices about their meals.

Practical Exercises and Recipes for Daily Life

Applying carbohydrate counting in everyday life can be challenging, but this section offers practical exercises and delicious recipes to make the process easier. From meal planning and grocery shopping tips to cooking techniques and recipe suggestions, individuals can gain confidence in incorporating carbohydrate counting into their daily routines. These exercises and recipes are designed to be accessible, enjoyable, and suitable for a wide range of dietary preferences.

In conclusion, "B. Carb-Counting" provides a comprehensive and detailed explanation of carbohydrate counting, its importance in managing diabetes, and maintaining balanced blood sugar levels. By covering various technical aspects such as the types of carbohydrates, the glycemic index, the significance of combining carbs with proteins and healthy fats, and the role of portion control, this guide equips individuals with the knowledge and tools necessary to take control of their blood sugar levels. With practical exercises and delicious recipes, individuals can confidently apply carbohydrate counting in their daily lives, leading to improved diabetes management and overall well-being.

CHAPTER 3: PROTEINS

In the context of a diabetic diet, proteins have numerous benefits. Firstly, proteins have a minimal impact on blood sugar levels compared to carbohydrates. This is beneficial for individuals with diabetes, as it helps in managing blood sugar levels and preventing sudden spikes or drops.

Secondly, proteins help in promoting satiety and reducing hunger cravings. This is particularly important for individuals with diabetes who need to manage their weight and control their calorie intake. Proteins take longer to digest, providing a longer-lasting feeling of fullness and helping to prevent overeating.

Furthermore, proteins play a crucial role in maintaining and repairing muscle tissues. Diabetes can lead to muscle wasting and weakness, and consuming adequate protein can help prevent these complications. Protein also supports the immune system, helping to fight off infections and promote overall health.

Including protein-rich meals in a diabetic diet is vital. Lean meats, poultry, fish, eggs, dairy products, lentils, and tofu are excellent sources of protein. It is important to choose lean proteins and avoid excessive intake of saturated fats to maintain a healthy diet.

Types of Protein

Proteins are essential macronutrients that play a vital role in a diabetic diet. They are crucial for maintaining overall health and managing blood sugar levels effectively. Unlike carbohydrates, proteins have a minimal impact on blood sugar, making them an excellent choice for individuals with diabetes. Additionally, proteins promote satiety, preventing overeating, and support muscle health and the immune system.

There are two types of proteins: animal proteins and plant proteins. Animal-based proteins come from meat, poultry, fish, eggs, and dairy products. These proteins are considered complete because they contain all of the amino acids necessary by the organism. Complete proteins are highly digestible and provide all the necessary building blocks for the body's protein synthesis.

Animal-based proteins offer several advantages for diabetics. They have a high biological value, meaning they provide a rich source of essential amino acids that the body needs for various functions. These proteins also tend to have a higher concentration of certain nutrients such as vitamin B12, iron, and zinc, which are important for overall health. However, it is essential to choose lean cuts of meat and low-fat dairy products to avoid excessive saturated fat intake.

On the other hand, plant-based proteins are derived from plant sources such as legumes, tofu, tempeh, seitan, and certain grains. While plant-based proteins may not be complete proteins individually, they can be combined to form complementary proteins that contain all the essential amino acids. This can be achieved by consuming a variety of plant-based protein sources throughout the day.

Plant-based proteins offer unique advantages for diabetics. They are often lower in saturated fat and cholesterol than animal-based proteins, making them heart-healthy options. Plant-based proteins are also rich in fiber, which aids in blood sugar management by slowing down digestion and preventing rapid spikes in blood sugar levels. Additionally, plant-based proteins are abundant in various vitamins, minerals, and phytochemicals that provide additional health benefits.

Incorporating both animal-based and plant-based proteins into a diabetic diet can provide a balanced and diverse range of nutrients. It is recommended to include a combination of lean meats, poultry, fish, eggs, dairy products, legumes, tofu, and other plant-based protein sources in the diet. This ensures an adequate intake of essential amino acids, while also benefiting from the unique advantages offered by each type of protein.

Balancing proteins in a diabetic diet is crucial for maintaining stable blood sugar levels and promoting overall health. There are two main types of proteins that can be incorporated into a diabetic diet: animal-based proteins and plant-based proteins.

It is important to consider portion sizes and cooking methods when consuming animal-based proteins to avoid excessive intake of saturated fat. Choosing lean cuts of meat, removing the skin from poultry, and opting for low-fat dairy products can help reduce the intake of unhealthy fats. When it comes to plant-based proteins, it is essential to ensure a variety of sources are included in the diet to obtain all the necessary amino acids.

By including a variety of protein sources in the diet, individuals with diabetes can ensure they are getting the necessary nutrients while managing their blood sugar effectively.

CHAPTER 4: FATS

Identifying Healthy Fats

Healthy fats are an essential component of a balanced diet for individuals with diabetes. They provide numerous health benefits and play a crucial role in managing blood sugar levels. Incorporating the right types of fats into your meals can help improve insulin sensitivity, reduce inflammation, and promote heart health.

There are several sources of healthy fats that you can include in your diet. These include:

1. Avocados: Avocados include monounsaturated fats, which can help lower bad cholesterol and lessen the risk of heart disease. They are also a good source of fiber, vitamins, and minerals.

2. Nuts and Seeds: Almonds, walnuts, chia seeds, flaxseeds, and hemp seeds are all excellent sources of healthy fats. They are also packed with protein, fiber, and antioxidants, making them a nutritious addition to your diet.

3. Olive Oil: Olive oil is a staple in Mediterranean cuisine and is known for its high content of monounsaturated fats. It can be used for cooking or as a dressing for salads and vegetables.

4. Fatty Fish: Fish such as salmon, mackerel, sardines, and trout are rich in omega-3 fatty acids, which have been shown to reduce inflammation and improve heart health. These fish are also a great source of protein.

5. Coconut Oil: Although it is high in saturated fat, coconut oil contains medium-chain triglycerides (MCTs) that can be beneficial for individuals with diabetes. MCTs are easy to digest and give an immediate source of energy.

Benefits of Healthy Fats in Diabetes Management

Incorporating healthy fats into your diet can have several benefits for individuals with diabetes. These include:

1. Blood Sugar Control: Healthy fats can help stabilize blood sugar levels by slowing down the absorption of carbohydrates. This can prevent spikes in blood sugar and promote better glycemic control.

2. Heart Health: Consuming healthy fats can promote heart health by lowering bad cholesterol levels while boosting good cholesterol levels. This can lower the risk of cardiovascular diseases, which are more common in individuals with diabetes.

3. Weight Management: Healthy fats are more satiating than carbohydrates, meaning they can help you feel fuller for longer. This can prevent overeating and aid in weight management, which is important for diabetes management.

4. Nutrient Absorption: Some vitamins, such as vitamins A, D, E, and K, are fat-soluble, which means they must be eaten with fat to be adequately absorbed by the body. Including healthy fats in your meals can ensure adequate absorption of these essential nutrients.

Recommended Daily Intake of Fats

The American Diabetes Association recommends that individuals with diabetes consume around 25-35% of their daily calories from fats. However, it is important to choose the right types of fats and consume them in moderation.

Limit your consumption of harmful fats, such as saturated and trans fats, as these can raise the risk of heart disease and aggravate insulin resistance. Unhealthy fats are frequently found in processed meals, fried foods, fatty cuts of meat, and full-fat dairy products.

Incorporating Healthy Fats into Your Diet

Here are some practical tips for incorporating healthy fats into your meals and snacks:

1. Use olive oil or avocado oil for cooking instead of butter or margarine.

2. Sprinkle nuts or seeds on top of salads, yogurt, or oatmeal.

3. Include fatty fish in your diet at least twice a week.

4. Snack on a handful of nuts or seeds instead of processed snacks.

5. Add sliced avocado to sandwiches, wraps, or salads.

6. Use natural nut butter (without added sugars) as a spread on whole grain bread or as a dip for fruits and vegetables.

By incorporating these sources of healthy fats into your diet and making mindful choices, you can optimize your nutrition and well-being while effectively managing your diabetes. Remember to get tailored counsel from a healthcare practitioner or qualified dietician.

Avoiding Unhealthy Fats

Unhealthy fats, such as saturated fats and trans fats, can have negative effects on our health. This sub-topic aims to help individuals identify these unhealthy fats and provides practical tips on how to limit their intake.

Saturated fats are commonly found in animal products like fatty cuts of meat, full-fat dairy products, and butter. These fats can raise cholesterol levels and increase the risk of heart disease. It is important to limit the consumption of saturated fats by choosing leaner cuts of meat, opting for low-fat or fat-free dairy products, and using healthier cooking methods like baking, grilling, or steaming.

Trans fats are artificial fats found in processed meals including fried dishes, packaged snacks, and baked products. These fats not only raise bad cholesterol levels but also lower good cholesterol levels, increasing the risk of heart disease. Reading food labels is crucial to identify trans fats, as they may be listed as "partially hydrogenated oils." It is best to avoid foods that contain trans fats altogether and opt for healthier alternatives.

To reduce the consumption of unhealthy fats, it is recommended to incorporate more plant-based fats into the diet. Avocados, nuts and seeds, olive oil, and coconut oil are examples of healthy fats that can be included in meals and snacks. These fats provide essential nutrients, promote heart health, and help control blood sugar levels. However, it is important to consume them in moderation, as they are still high in calories.

When choosing cooking oils, it is best to opt for healthier options like olive oil, canola oil, or avocado oil. These oils are rich in monounsaturated fats, which are beneficial for heart health. It is also important to limit the use of butter, lard, and other solid fats in cooking and baking.

Reading food labels is essential in identifying the presence of unhealthy fats in packaged foods. Look for products that are labeled as "low in saturated fat" or "trans fat-free." Additionally, be cautious of foods that contain partially hydrogenated oils, as they often indicate the presence of trans fats.

Incorporating more whole foods into the diet, such as fruits, vegetables, whole grains, and lean proteins, can also help reduce the consumption of unhealthy fats. These foods are naturally low in unhealthy fats and provide essential nutrients for overall health.

It is always recommended to consult with a healthcare professional or registered dietitian for personalized advice and guidance on incorporating healthy fats into a balanced diet.

CHAPTER 5: FIBER'S ROLE IN DIABETES CONTROL

In addition to blood sugar control, fiber also improves insulin sensitivity. Insulin is the hormone responsible for transporting glucose from the bloodstream into the cells for energy. By improving insulin sensitivity, fiber helps the body use insulin more effectively, ensuring that glucose is properly utilized and preventing insulin resistance.

Furthermore, a high-fiber diet can reduce the risk of developing complications associated with diabetes. Fiber aids in weight management by promoting a feeling of fullness and reducing calorie intake. This can be particularly beneficial for individuals with diabetes who may need to manage their weight to improve blood sugar control. Additionally, fiber helps lower cholesterol levels and promotes healthy digestion, reducing the risk of heart disease and gastrointestinal issues commonly seen in people with diabetes.

The recommended daily intake of fiber varies depending on age, gender, and overall health. For adults, the typical suggestion is to ingest between 25 and 38 grams of fiber daily. To reduce stomach pain, it is recommended to increase fiber consumption gradually.

There are two kinds of dietary fiber: soluble and insoluble. Soluble fiber dissolves in water to produce a gel-like material in the digestive system. Fruits, vegetables, legumes, and cereals are excellent sources of soluble fiber. Insoluble fiber, on the other hand, bulks up the stool and helps avoid constipation. Whole grains, nuts, seeds, and bran are examples of foods high in insoluble fiber.

Incorporating fiber into a diabetes-friendly diet can be done in various ways. Including more fruits and vegetables in meals and snacks is an easy way to increase fiber intake. Opting for whole grain products such as whole wheat bread, brown rice, and whole grain pasta instead of refined grains is another way to add more fiber. Snacking on nuts, seeds, and legumes can also contribute to a higher fiber intake.

High-Fiber Foods

Maintaining stable blood sugar levels is crucial for overall health, especially for individuals with conditions such as diabetes. One effective way to regulate blood sugar levels is by incorporating high-fiber foods into our diets. In this article, we will explore the importance of high-fiber foods in blood sugar control, provide a comprehensive list of fiber-rich foods, and explain how these foods aid in regulating blood sugar levels.

Importance of High-Fiber Foods in Blood Sugar Control

High-fiber foods play a vital role in managing blood sugar levels due to their unique properties. Fiber, a type of carbohydrate that cannot be digested by the body, slows down the absorption of glucose into the bloodstream. This slower absorption prevents sudden spikes in blood sugar levels, promoting more stable and controlled glucose levels.

Furthermore, high-fiber foods help improve insulin sensitivity. Insulin is a hormone responsible for regulating blood sugar levels by facilitating the absorption of glucose into cells. By consuming fiber-rich foods, the body becomes more responsive to insulin, allowing for better glucose utilization and regulation.

List of Fiber-Rich Foods

Including a variety of fiber-rich foods in our diet is essential for reaping the benefits of blood sugar control. Here is a comprehensive list of high-fiber foods:

1. Whole Grains: Include healthy grains like oats, brown rice, quinoa, and whole wheat bread in your meals. These grains are rich in fiber, vitamins, and minerals, making them an excellent choice for maintaining stable blood sugar levels.

2. Legumes: Beans, lentils, chickpeas, and other legumes are high in fiber and a good source of plant protein. Including legumes in your diet can help regulate blood sugar levels while providing essential nutrients.

3. Fruits: Opt for fruits such as apples, berries, pears, and oranges, which are rich in fiber. Consuming whole fruits instead of fruit juices ensures that you benefit from the natural fiber content.

4. Vegetables: Incorporate a variety of vegetables like broccoli, Brussels sprouts, carrots, and leafy greens into your meals. These vegetables are not only high in fiber but also packed with essential vitamins and minerals.

5. Nuts and Seeds: Almonds, chia seeds, flaxseeds, and walnuts are excellent sources of fiber and healthy fats. Adding a handful of nuts or seeds to your diet provides a satisfying crunch while boosting your fiber intake.

How High-Fiber Foods Aid in Regulating Blood Sugar Levels

High-fiber foods aid in blood sugar control through various mechanisms. Firstly, the slow digestion and absorption of fiber-rich foods prevent sudden spikes in blood sugar levels. Instead, glucose is released gradually into the bloodstream, avoiding the need for excessive insulin production.

Furthermore, fiber induces satiety, which helps to manage appetite and prevent overeating. By feeling satisfied for longer periods of time, you are less likely to ingest excessive amounts of carbs, which can contribute to blood sugar abnormalities. Moreover, the fermentation of fiber in the gut produces short-chain fatty acids, which play a role in improving insulin sensitivity. These fatty acids help the body utilize glucose more efficiently, further assisting in blood sugar regulation.

By making these dietary changes, you can take a proactive step towards maintaining stable blood sugar levels and promoting overall health.

Incorporating Fiber

Incorporating fiber into your daily meals is crucial for managing diabetes. High-fiber meals help to regulate blood sugar levels by delaying carbohydrate digestion and absorption, which prevents blood sugar rises. They also offer numerous health benefits, including improved insulin sensitivity, weight management, lower cholesterol levels, and support for healthy digestion.

To improve your fiber intake, eat a variety of fruits, vegetables, legumes, whole grains, nuts, and seeds. These foods are excellent sources of dietary fiber and can easily be incorporated into your meals.

One way to increase fiber intake is by adding more fruits to your diet. Fruits such as berries, apples, pears, and oranges are rich in fiber. They may be enjoyed as snacks, added to morning cereals or yogurt, or included into salads and smoothies.

Vegetables are another essential source of fiber. Include a variety of vegetables like broccoli, spinach, carrots, and Brussels sprouts in your meals. You can steam or roast them as side dishes, add them to stir-fries, or include them in soups and stews.

Whole grains are an excellent choice for increasing fiber intake. Choose whole wheat bread, brown rice, quinoa, and oats over processed grains. These whole grains may be used in a variety of dishes, including salads, pilafs, and as an alternative to refined grains in baking.

Legumes, which include beans, lentils, and chickpeas, are high in both fiber and protein. Incorporate them into your meals by making bean-based soups, adding them to salads, or preparing delicious bean burgers.

Portion control is essential when incorporating fiber into your meals. While fiber is good, ingesting too much might create stomach issues. Gradually increase your fiber intake, and drink plenty of water to aid digestion and prevent any discomfort.

Meal planning is another helpful strategy. Plan your meals in advance, ensuring that each meal includes a good source of fiber. This can help you stay on track and make healthier choices throughout the day.

To make your meals more enjoyable and flavorful, explore recipes that are rich in fiber. Look for recipes that incorporate a variety of high-fiber ingredients and experiment with different flavors and cooking techniques. This will help you discover new and exciting ways to incorporate fiber into your meals.

By following these practical suggestions and making fiber-rich foods a regular part of your diet, you can take a significant step towards better diabetes management and overall health.

CHAPTER 6: VITAMINS AND MINERALS ESSENTIAL FOR DIABETICS

Key Nutrients

The key nutrients play a crucial role in managing diabetes and promoting overall health in individuals with this condition. By understanding the importance of these nutrients and incorporating them into their diet, individuals with diabetes can effectively manage their blood sugar levels and support their overall well-being.

One essential nutrient for individuals with diabetes is vitamin D. This vitamin is known for its role in bone health, but it also plays a significant role in regulating blood sugar levels. Vitamin D helps improve insulin sensitivity, which is important for individuals with diabetes. It also supports immune function and helps reduce inflammation in the body. Fatty seafood such as salmon and mackerel, fortified dairy products, and exposure to sunshine are all good sources of vitamin D.

Another important nutrient for individuals with diabetes is magnesium. Magnesium is involved in over 300 biochemical reactions in the body, including the metabolism of carbohydrates and the regulation of insulin. It helps improve insulin sensitivity and may also contribute to better blood sugar control. Leafy green vegetables, nuts and seeds, whole grains, and legumes are excellent sources of magnesium in the diet. Vitamin C is also good to diabetics. This vitamin is well-known for its antioxidant qualities, which serve to protect the body from free radical damage. Vitamin C also improves immune function and wound healing, which is especially essential for diabetics who may have poor wound healing. Citrus fruits, strawberries, kiwi, and bell peppers are excellent sources of vitamin C.

Zinc is another important nutrient for individuals with diabetes. It plays a role in insulin production and release, as well as in the metabolism of carbohydrates. Zinc also supports immune function and helps with wound healing. Good dietary sources of zinc include oysters, beef, poultry, nuts, and legumes.

Chromium is a trace mineral that is essential for carbohydrate and lipid metabolism. It helps improve insulin sensitivity and may also contribute to better blood sugar control. Broccoli, healthy grains, and lean meat are good sources of chromium.

Incorporating these key nutrients into a diabetic-friendly diet is essential for managing diabetes and promoting overall health. This cannot be emphasized enough: it is important to focus on a balanced diet that includes a variety of nutrient-rich foods. This includes consuming a mix of carbohydrates, proteins, and fats in appropriate portions to help manage blood sugar levels. Controlling portion sizes and eating whole, unadulterated foods can help diabetics maintain a balanced diet.

It is recommended that individuals with diabetes work with a healthcare professional or a registered dietitian to determine their specific nutrient needs and develop a personalized meal plan. They can provide guidance on the recommended daily intake of these key nutrients and help individuals incorporate them into their diet in a practical and sustainable way.

In conclusion, understanding the role of key nutrients in managing diabetes is crucial for individuals with this condition. By incorporating essential vitamins and minerals like vitamin D, magnesium, vitamin C, zinc, and chromium into their diet, individuals with diabetes can effectively manage their blood sugar levels, support their immune function, and promote overall health. A balanced diet that includes a variety of nutrient-rich foods is essential for individuals with diabetes to maintain optimal health.

Nutrient-Dense Foods

Nutrient-dense foods play a crucial role in managing diabetes and promoting overall health. These foods are rich in essential nutrients such as vitamins, minerals, and antioxidants that are vital for maintaining optimal health and well-being. Incorporating nutrient-dense foods into a diabetic diet can help regulate blood sugar levels, improve insulin sensitivity, and support immune function.

One important nutrient for individuals with diabetes is vitamin D. This nutrient has been shown to improve insulin sensitivity, which is beneficial for managing blood sugar levels. Additionally, vitamin D plays a role in supporting immune function, which is essential for individuals with diabetes who may have a compromised immune system. Some food sources of vitamin D include fatty fish like salmon and mackerel, fortified dairy products, and egg yolks.

Another vital nutrient for diabetes management is magnesium. This mineral is involved in regulating insulin and blood sugar levels. Adequate magnesium intake has been associated with improved insulin sensitivity and better blood sugar control. Foods high in magnesium include leafy green vegetables, nuts & seeds, whole grains, and legumes.

Vitamin C is also important for individuals with diabetes. This antioxidant vitamin helps protect against free radicals, which can cause damage to cells and contribute to chronic diseases. Vitamin C also plays a role in wound healing, which is especially significant for those with diabetes, who may have delayed healing rates. Citrus fruits, strawberries, kiwi, and bell peppers are rich in vitamin C.

Zinc is another nutrient that plays a crucial role in diabetes management. It is involved in insulin production and helps support immune function. Including zinc-rich foods in the diet can help enhance insulin sensitivity and support overall health. Good sources of zinc include lean meats, seafood, whole grains, and legumes.

Incorporating nutrient-dense foods into a diabetic diet can be done in various ways. One approach is to focus on consuming a variety of fruits and vegetables, aiming for at least five servings per day. These should include a mix of colorful fruits and vegetables to ensure a wide range of nutrients. Additionally, incorporating lean proteins such as poultry, fish, and tofu can provide essential nutrients while keeping saturated fat intake in check.

Whole grains, such as quinoa, brown rice, and whole wheat bread, are excellent sources of fiber and important nutrients. Including these in the diet can help regulate blood sugar levels and provide sustained energy throughout the day. Nuts and seeds, such as almonds, walnuts, and chia seeds, are also nutrient-dense foods that can be incorporated into meals and snacks.

It is crucial to remember that individual nutrient requirements vary, thus it is advised that you consult with a healthcare practitioner or certified dietitian to create a specific meal plan. They may advise on portion amounts, meal timing, and nutrient requirements depending on personal needs and goals.

By including a variety of nutrient-rich foods in the diet, individuals with diabetes can optimize their health and well-being.

CHAPTER 7: GLYCEMIC INDEX AND DIABETES

Glycemic Index Explained

The glycemic index (GI) is a measurement that determines how quickly carbohydrates in food raise blood sugar levels. It plays a crucial role in blood sugar management, especially for individuals with diabetes. Understanding the glycemic index is essential for maintaining stable blood sugar levels and reducing the risk of complications.

The GI is calculated by comparing the blood sugar response to a specific food to the response of a standard reference food, usually pure glucose or white bread. Foods with a high GI value, such as white bread or sugary snacks, cause a rapid increase in blood sugar levels. On the other hand, foods with a low GI value, like whole grains, legumes, non-starchy vegetables, and low-sugar fruits, result in a slower and more gradual rise in blood sugar levels.

Incorporating low GI foods into a diabetic meal plan is important because it helps prevent blood sugar spikes and promotes better blood sugar control. When we consume high GI foods, our bodies quickly break down the carbohydrates into glucose, causing a sudden increase in blood sugar levels. This can be problematic for individuals with diabetes, as their bodies may struggle to produce enough insulin or utilize it effectively.

By choosing low GI foods, individuals can maintain a more stable blood sugar level throughout the day. This is because low-GI meals digest and absorb more slowly, resulting in a slower and more regulated release of glucose into the circulation. As a result, insulin can be more effectively utilized, preventing sudden spikes or drops in blood sugar levels.

In addition to blood sugar management, the glycemic index can also be beneficial for weight management. Foods with a lower GI value tend to be more filling and can help control appetite, leading to better portion control and weight management.

It is important to note that the glycemic index is just one factor to consider when planning a healthy diet. Other factors, such as portion sizes, overall carbohydrate intake, and the combination of different foods in a meal, also play a role in blood sugar management.

By choosing low GI foods, individuals can promote better blood sugar control and overall health.

Low Glycemic Choices

Low glycemic choices are an essential component of a healthy meal plan, particularly for individuals with diabetes or those looking to manage their blood sugar levels. These foods have a lower glycemic index (GI), which, to reiterate, means they cause a slower and more gradual rise in blood sugar compared to high GI foods. Incorporating low GI foods into your diet can help maintain stable blood sugar levels and promote overall health.

Here is a list of low glycemic choices that you can consider when planning your meals:

1. Whole grains: Opt for whole grain options such as brown rice, quinoa, and whole wheat bread instead of refined grains. These provide more fiber and nutrients, resulting in a lower GI.

2. Legumes: Include legumes like lentils, chickpeas, and kidney beans in your meals. They are high in fiber and protein, making them excellent low GI choices.

3. Non-starchy vegetables: Load up on non-starchy vegetables like broccoli, spinach, cauliflower, and peppers. These vegetables are low in carbohydrates and have a minimal impact on blood sugar levels.

4. Fruits: Choose fruits with a lower GI such as berries, cherries, apples, and pears. These fruits contain fiber and are packed with vitamins and minerals.

5. Lean proteins: Incorporate lean sources of protein like skinless chicken, turkey, fish, tofu, and eggs into your meals. Protein-rich foods have a minimal effect on blood sugar levels.

6. Healthy fats: Include healthy fat sources in your diet, such as avocados, nuts, and seeds. These foods provide essential nutrients and help slow down the digestion of carbohydrates, resulting in a lower GI.

7. Dairy products: Opt for low-fat dairy products such as Greek yogurt, skim milk, and cottage cheese. These provide protein and calcium without causing a significant rise in blood sugar.

When incorporating low glycemic choices into your meals, here are some tips to keep in mind:

• Aim for a balanced plate: Include a combination of low GI foods from different food groups to ensure a well-rounded meal.

• Pay attention to portion sizes: Even though a food may have a low GI, consuming large portions can still impact blood sugar levels. Be mindful of portion sizes to maintain stable blood sugar control.

• Combine with high fiber foods: Pairing low GI foods with high fiber foods can further slow down the absorption of glucose, promoting better blood sugar management.

• Be mindful of cooking methods: Opt for healthier cooking methods such as steaming, grilling, or baking instead of frying to maintain the nutritional value of low GI foods.

By making these healthier food choices, you can take a proactive approach to managing your blood sugar levels and promoting overall well-being.

CHAPTER 8: COMPREHENSIVE FOOD LISTS FOR DIABETICS

Beans

Beans are an excellent source of dietary fiber, which plays a crucial role in managing blood sugar levels. Beans' high fiber content slows carbohydrate absorption, minimizing blood glucose rises. This is particularly beneficial for individuals with diabetes, as it promotes better glycemic control.

Furthermore, beans are a rich source of protein, making them an ideal choice for individuals following a plant-based or vegetarian diet. Protein is essential for building and repairing tissues, and it also helps to stabilize blood sugar levels. Incorporating beans into meals can provide diabetics with a sustainable source of protein, aiding in overall health and well-being.

In addition to fiber and protein, beans are packed with essential vitamins and minerals. They are an excellent source of folate, magnesium, and potassium, which are all important for maintaining optimal health. Folate is essential for red blood cell production and helps prevent certain birth defects. Magnesium plays a vital role in regulating blood pressure and blood sugar levels, while potassium helps maintain healthy heart function.

Moreover, beans have a low glycemic index, meaning they have a minimal impact on blood sugar levels. This makes them an ideal food choice for diabetics, as they can be included in meals without causing significant fluctuations in glucose levels.

The versatility of beans also makes them an excellent addition to a diabetic-friendly diet. They may be used in soups, salads, stews, and even desserts. Whether it's black beans, kidney beans, chickpeas, or lentils, there are several ways to incorporate beans into a diabetic diet plan.

A. Kidney Beans

Kidney beans are a powerhouse of nutrition and offer numerous benefits for individuals managing diabetes. These small, kidney-shaped legumes are not only packed with essential nutrients but also have a low glycemic index, making them an excellent choice for those with diabetes.

One of the standout features of kidney beans is their high fiber content. Fiber plays a crucial role in regulating blood sugar levels and improving digestion. By slowing down the absorption of carbohydrates, kidney beans help prevent spikes in blood sugar, providing a steady release of energy throughout the day. This makes them a perfect snack for anyone trying to control their diabetes properly.

In addition to their fiber content, kidney beans are rich in healthy fats and lean protein. These nutrients are essential for maintaining overall health and well-being. The healthy fats found in kidney beans contribute to heart health and provide a source of sustained energy. Meanwhile, the lean protein content helps build and repair tissues, supporting muscle strength and development.

Kidney beans are also a treasure trove of vitamins and minerals that are beneficial for individuals with diabetes. They are an excellent source of folate, which is essential for red blood cell production and DNA synthesis. Iron, another key nutrient found in kidney beans, helps prevent anemia and supports the transport of oxygen throughout the body. Magnesium, on the other hand, plays a role in regulating blood pressure and blood sugar levels. Lastly, kidney beans are a good source of potassium, which aids in maintaining proper nerve and muscle function.

When incorporating kidney beans into a diabetic-friendly diet, portion control is important. While individual needs may vary, a general guideline is to consume about ½ cup of cooked kidney beans per serving. This provides approximately 20 grams of carbohydrates, 8 grams of fiber, and 7 grams of protein. It's worth noting that kidney beans have a low glycemic index, meaning they have a minimal impact on blood sugar levels when consumed in moderation.

To fully reap the benefits of kidney beans, it's essential to incorporate them into a well-balanced diet. There are countless delicious and nutritious recipes that feature kidney beans as a star ingredient. From hearty soups and stews to flavorful salads and dips, the versatility of kidney beans allows for endless culinary possibilities. Whether you're aiming to control your blood sugar levels or simply looking to enhance your overall health, kidney beans are a valuable addition to any diabetic-friendly meal plan.

In conclusion, kidney beans are a nutritious and beneficial food for individuals managing diabetes. Their high fiber content, low glycemic index, and abundance of essential nutrients make them an excellent choice for blood sugar regulation and overall health. By incorporating kidney beans into a well-balanced diet, individuals can enjoy their versatility and reap the numerous benefits they offer. So go ahead, embrace the deliciousness and nourishment that kidney beans bring to the table.

B. Pinto Beans

Pinto beans, a type of legume cherished in various cuisines worldwide, offer not only delectable flavors, but also a plethora of health benefits, particularly for individuals managing diabetes. These humble legumes possess a remarkable nutritional profile that aids in blood sugar control and overall well-being.

One of the key advantages of pinto beans for individuals with diabetes is their low glycemic index. Unlike high glycemic foods that cause a rapid spike in blood sugar levels, pinto beans induce a slower and more controlled rise. This makes them an ideal choice for controlling blood sugar levels and treating diabetes.

Beyond their impact on blood sugar, pinto beans are rich in complex carbohydrates. These carbohydrates are digested slowly, resulting in a minimal impact on blood sugar levels while providing a steady and sustained source of energy. This characteristic is particularly beneficial for individuals with diabetes, as it helps prevent sudden spikes and crashes in blood sugar levels.

Another standout feature of pinto beans is their impressive fiber content. Fiber plays a vital role in diabetes management by aiding in blood sugar control, improving digestion, and promoting a feeling of fullness, which helps prevent overeating. Incorporating pinto beans into your diet can contribute to a healthier digestive system and assist in maintaining a balanced blood sugar profile.

In addition to their fiber content, pinto beans contain healthy fats, including omega-3 and omega-6 fatty acids. These essential fats have been linked to improved heart health, making pinto beans a heart-friendly choice for individuals with diabetes. Furthermore, pinto beans offer a moderate amount of lean protein, making them an ideal option for those seeking to incorporate plant-based protein into their diet.

When it comes to essential vitamins and minerals, pinto beans are a nutritional powerhouse. They are particularly rich in folate, iron, magnesium, and potassium. Folate is crucial for red blood cell production, iron supports oxygen transportation throughout the body, magnesium aids in blood sugar regulation, and potassium plays a vital role in maintaining healthy blood pressure levels. By including pinto beans in your meals, you can fortify your body with these essential nutrients, supporting overall health and effectively managing diabetes.

To reap the benefits of pinto beans without compromising portion control, it is recommended to consume approximately ½ cup of cooked pinto beans per serving. When deciding portion sizes, individual demands and dietary restrictions must be taken into account.

In summary, pinto beans are a remarkable addition to the diet of individuals managing diabetes. With their low glycemic index, complex carbohydrates, high fiber content, healthy fats, moderate lean protein content, and abundance of key vitamins and minerals, pinto beans offer a comprehensive nutritional package. By incorporating these versatile legumes into your meals in appropriate portions, you can harness their potential to support blood sugar control, heart health, and overall well-being.

C. Navy Beans

Navy beans, a type of small, white beans, are a versatile ingredient found in various cuisines. They not only add flavor and texture to dishes but also offer numerous health benefits, particularly for individuals managing diabetes. Navy beans, with their low glycemic index and high fiber content, help to regulate blood sugar levels.

One of the key advantages of navy beans is their ability to slow down the absorption of glucose in the bloodstream. This helps prevent spikes in blood sugar levels and promotes stable glycemic control. Moreover, navy beans are an excellent source of plant-based protein, making them an ideal choice for those seeking to increase their lean protein intake. Incorporating navy beans into a well-balanced diet can support overall health and well-being.

Navy beans are also rich in dietary fiber, with approximately 19 grams per cup. This high fiber content aids in digestion and promotes a feeling of fullness, making navy beans a valuable food for weight management. Furthermore, the fiber in navy beans contributes to regulating blood sugar levels and reducing the risk of heart disease.

In terms of nutritional composition, navy beans have a low glycemic index, meaning they have a minimal impact on blood sugar levels. They are a wonderful source of carbs, giving steady energy without producing blood sugar spikes. Additionally, navy beans are low in fat and contain mainly healthy fats, including omega-3 fatty acids, which are beneficial for heart health.

Not only are navy beans packed with fiber and healthy fats, but they also offer an impressive amount of plant-based protein. With around 15 grams of protein per cup, navy beans are an excellent choice for individuals looking to meet their protein needs without relying on animal sources.

In addition to their macronutrient content, navy beans are rich in essential vitamins and minerals. They are particularly high in folate, iron, magnesium, and potassium, all of which contribute to overall health and well-being.

When incorporating navy beans into a diabetic diet, it is important to consider portion control. A recommended portion size of navy beans is about 1/2 to 1 cup, depending on individual dietary needs. This ensures that the beans' nutritional benefits are maximized while maintaining a balanced meal plan.

In conclusion, navy beans are an excellent complement to any diet, particularly for people with diabetes. Their low glycemic index, high fiber content, and plant-based protein make them an excellent choice for blood sugar regulation, weight management, and overall health. By including navy beans in your meals, you can enjoy their delicious taste while reaping the numerous nutritional benefits they offer.

D. Black Beans

Black beans are an excellent choice for diabetic health management due to their numerous benefits. They are a rich source of fiber, which helps regulate blood sugar levels and improve insulin sensitivity. Additionally, black beans have a low glycemic index, meaning they cause a slower rise in blood sugar levels compared to other carbohydrate-rich foods. This makes them a great option for maintaining stable blood sugar levels.

In terms of nutritional content, black beans are packed with essential nutrients. They are a good source of carbohydrates, providing a steady release of energy without causing spikes in blood sugar. They are also high in fiber, which aids in digestion and helps control appetite. Black beans include healthful lipids, including omega-3 fatty acids, which are good for your heart. They are also high in lean protein, making them suitable for vegetarians and vegans.

In addition to their macronutrient content, black beans are loaded with key vitamins and minerals. They are a rich source of folate, which is important for red blood cell production and fetal development. They also include iron, magnesium, and potassium, which are required for a variety of biological activities. Black beans are also high in antioxidants, which help prevent oxidative stress and inflammation.

Recommended portion sizes of black beans vary depending on individual needs and dietary preferences. However, a general guideline is to consume around 1/2 to 1 cup of cooked black beans per serving. It is important to note that portion control is crucial, as excessive consumption of black beans may lead to digestive discomfort.

Key Nutritional Information:

- Glycemic Index: Low
- Carbohydrate Content: Approximately 40 grams per cup
- Fiber Content: Approximately 15 grams per cup
- Healthy Fats: Including omega-3 fatty acids
- Lean Protein Content: Approximately 15 grams per cup
- Key Vitamins and Minerals: Folate, iron, magnesium, potassium, antioxidants

By incorporating black beans into a diabetic diet, individuals can enjoy their numerous health benefits while managing their blood sugar levels effectively.

Dark Green Leafy Vegetables

One of the key advantages of dark green leafy vegetables is their high antioxidant content. Antioxidants help reduce inflammation in the body and improve insulin sensitivity, which is crucial for individuals with diabetes. By incorporating these vegetables into their diet, individuals can effectively control their blood sugar levels and reduce the risk of complications associated with diabetes.

In addition to their blood sugar management benefits, dark green leafy vegetables also promote overall health. They contribute to a well-balanced diet and provide a wide range of vitamins and minerals, including vitamin K, vitamin C, calcium, and iron. These nutrients are essential for maintaining a healthy body and supporting optimal bodily functions.

A. Spinach

Spinach is a leafy green vegetable that holds immense value for individuals with diabetes, as it offers a range of health benefits. This nutrient-dense vegetable is not only packed with essential nutrients but also possesses a low glycemic index, making it an ideal choice for those looking to effectively manage their blood sugar levels.

One of the key advantages of spinach is its high dietary fiber content. Fiber helps to regulate blood sugar levels and improve insulin sensitivity. By slowing down the absorption of glucose in the bloodstream, spinach helps prevent sudden spikes in blood sugar levels, making it a valuable addition to a diabetic-friendly diet.

Furthermore, spinach is low in carbohydrates and calories, making it an excellent option for individuals who are conscious of their weight. Its low carbohydrate content ensures that it has a minimal impact on blood sugar levels, while its low-calorie nature aids in weight management, a crucial aspect of diabetes control.

In addition to its favorable macronutrient profile, spinach boasts an impressive array of micronutrients. It is rich in key vitamins and minerals, including vitamin A, vitamin C, vitamin K, iron, and magnesium. These nutrients are essential for maintaining overall health and wellbeing, and they play a vital role in supporting various bodily functions.

Spinach also contains healthy fats and provides a moderate amount of lean protein. These nutrients are important for individuals with diabetes, as they contribute to satiety and help maintain stable blood sugar levels. Incorporating spinach into meals can provide a well-rounded nutritional profile, ensuring that individuals with diabetes meet their dietary requirements.

When it comes to portion sizes, it is important to consider individual needs and dietary requirements. However, a general guideline suggests consuming around 1 to 2 cups of cooked spinach per serving. This portion size allows for an adequate intake of the vegetable's beneficial nutrients without overwhelming the meal.

To make the most of spinach's nutritional content, it is advisable to incorporate it into a variety of dishes. Spinach can be eaten in salads, smoothies, stir-fries, soups, or as a side dish. Its adaptability provides for unlimited culinary choices, guaranteeing that those with diabetes may enjoy its advantages in a variety of meals.

When storing spinach, it is essential to keep it fresh and crisp. To achieve this, it is recommended to store spinach in the refrigerator, preferably in a sealed bag or container to maintain its moisture. It is important to note that spinach is best consumed within a few days of purchase to ensure optimal freshness and nutrient content.

In conclusion, spinach is a highly beneficial vegetable for individuals with diabetes. Its low glycemic index, low carbohydrate content, and high fiber content make it an excellent choice for managing blood sugar levels. Additionally, spinach provides healthy fats, lean protein, and a range of essential vitamins and minerals, further supporting overall health and wellbeing. By incorporating spinach into meals and following recommended portion sizes, individuals with diabetes can harness the numerous advantages this leafy green offers.

B. Collards

Collards, a nutritious leafy green vegetable, offer numerous benefits for individuals managing diabetes. With their low calorie and carbohydrate content, collards are an excellent choice for those looking to maintain stable blood sugar levels. Additionally, the high fiber content in collards aids in regulating blood sugar and improving digestion. These greens also contain healthy fats and lean protein, contributing to overall health and satiety.

One of the key advantages of collards for diabetic health management is their low glycemic index. This means that consuming collards has minimal impact on blood sugar levels, making them a favorable option for individuals with diabetes. Furthermore, collards are low in carbohydrates, making them suitable for those following a low-carb or diabetic diet.

The high fiber content in collards is particularly beneficial for individuals with diabetes. Fiber helps to manage blood sugar levels by decreasing the absorption of glucose in the blood. It also increases a sensation of fullness, which can help with weight management.

Collards contain beneficial lipids, such as omega-3 fatty acids. These fats have been shown to improve insulin sensitivity and reduce inflammation, both of which are important for managing diabetes and reducing the risk of complications.

In terms of protein content, collards provide a moderate amount of lean protein. Protein is essential for muscle growth and repair, and including it in meals can help balance blood sugar levels.

In addition to their nutritional benefits, collards are rich in vitamins and minerals. They are particularly high in vitamins A, C, and K, which contribute to immune function, skin health, and blood clotting. Collards also contain minerals such as calcium, iron, and magnesium, which are important for bone health, oxygen transport, and nerve function.

When consuming collards, it is important to be mindful of portion sizes. A serving size of cooked collards is typically around 1 cup. As always, it is recommended to consult with a healthcare professional or registered dietitian for personalized dietary recommendations that suit your specific needs.

Remember, the information provided here is for educational purposes only and should not be considered as medical advice. Always visit a healthcare practitioner for tailored diabetes management advice.

C. Kale

Kale is a leafy green vegetable that offers numerous benefits for individuals managing diabetes. It is a nutrient-dense food that can be incorporated into a diabetic diet to support overall health and blood sugar management. Here is a detailed description of kale and its benefits for diabetic health management:

- Glycemic index: Kale has a low glycemic index, which means it does not cause a rapid increase in blood sugar levels. This makes it a suitable choice for individuals with diabetes who need to monitor their blood sugar levels.
- Carbohydrate content: Kale is low in carbohydrates, making it an excellent option for diabetics who need to manage their carbohydrate intake. It delivers vital nutrients without dramatically affecting blood glucose levels.
- Fiber content: Kale is rich in fiber, which is beneficial for individuals with diabetes. Fiber regulates blood sugar levels by decreasing the absorption of glucose in the circulation. It also promotes healthy digestion and can contribute to a feeling of fullness.
- Healthy fats: While kale is not a significant source of fat, it does contain small amounts of healthy fats, including omega-3 fatty acids. These fats are beneficial for heart health and can improve insulin sensitivity, reducing the risk of complications associated with diabetes.
- Lean protein content: Although kale is not a significant source of protein, it does contain some amount of this macronutrient. Protein is essential for muscle growth and repair, as well as balancing blood sugar levels. Combining kale with other protein sources can help create a balanced meal for individuals with diabetes.
- Key vitamins and minerals: Kale is a powerhouse of vitamins and minerals that are essential for overall health and wellbeing. It is particularly rich in vitamins A, C, and K. Vitamin A supports eye health, vitamin C boosts the immune system, and vitamin K plays a role in blood clotting. Kale also provides minerals such as calcium, iron, and magnesium, which are important for bone health, oxygen transport, and energy production.
- Recommended portion sizes: When incorporating kale into a diabetic diet, it is important to be mindful of portion sizes. It is recommended to consume one to two cups of kale per serving,

depending on individual dietary needs. Consulting with a healthcare expert or registered dietician can give individualized advice based on your unique health objectives and needs.

Incorporating kale into a diabetic diet can provide a range of health benefits. Its low glycemic index, low carbohydrate content, high fiber content, and abundance of essential vitamins and minerals make it an excellent choice for blood sugar management and overall health. Adding kale to salads, soups, stir-fries, or smoothies can be a delicious and nutritious way to support diabetic health management.

Citrus Fruits

One of the key benefits of citrus fruits for diabetes management is their low glycemic index. This means that they have a minimal impact on blood sugar levels compared to other fruits and foods high in carbohydrates. Citrus fruits such as oranges, grapefruits, and lemons have a low glycemic index, making them a suitable choice for individuals with diabetes.

Citrus fruits are also rich in dietary fiber, which is beneficial for diabetes management. Fiber helps to decrease the absorption of sugar into the circulation, reducing blood sugar rises. Additionally, fiber promotes satiety and can help control appetite, making it easier for individuals with diabetes to manage their weight.

Furthermore, citrus fruits are an excellent source of vitamin C, a powerful antioxidant that plays a crucial role in supporting overall health. Vitamin C helps strengthen the immune system, reduces inflammation, and promotes wound healing, which is particularly important for individuals with diabetes who may have a compromised immune system.

In addition to vitamin C, citrus fruits also contain other essential vitamins and minerals, such as potassium and folate. Potassium helps to control blood pressure and promotes heart health. Folate is needed for cell growth and development, making it especially critical for diabetic pregnant women.

Including citrus fruits in a balanced diet can provide numerous health benefits for individuals with diabetes. However, it is important to consume them in moderation and as part of an overall healthy eating plan. It is always advisable to consult with a healthcare professional or a registered dietitian for personalized guidance on incorporating citrus fruits into a diabetes management plan.

A. Grapefruits

Grapefruits are citrus fruits that are known for their tart and tangy flavor. They are an excellent choice for diabetic health management due to their low glycemic index and high fiber content. Incorporating grapefruits into a diabetic-friendly diet can provide numerous benefits, including regulating blood sugar levels, improving insulin sensitivity, and reducing the risk of complications associated with diabetes.

Let's explore the key nutritional information about grapefruits:

- Glycemic Index: Grapefruits have a low glycemic index, which means they have a minimal impact on blood sugar levels. This makes them a suitable fruit choice for individuals with diabetes who need to manage their blood sugar.
- Carbohydrate Content: A medium-sized grapefruit contains approximately 20 grams of carbohydrates. It's important for individuals with diabetes to be aware of their carbohydrate intake, as it directly affects blood sugar levels. Grapefruits can be included in a well-balanced meal plan, taking into account the total carbohydrate content.
- Fiber Content: Grapefruits are high in fiber, with an average medium-sized fruit providing around 4 grams of fiber. Fiber is beneficial for individuals with diabetes as it helps slow down the absorption of sugar into the bloodstream, promoting better blood sugar control.
- Healthy Fats: Grapefruits are low in fat and do not contain unhealthy saturated or trans fats. This makes them a heart-healthy choice for individuals with diabetes, as they can help maintain healthy cholesterol levels.
- Lean Protein Content: Grapefruits contain some protein, but not much. Protein is crucial for sustaining muscle mass and promoting general health. Individuals with diabetes can incorporate other protein sources into their meals to ensure a balanced diet.
- Key Vitamins and Minerals: Grapefruits are rich in vitamin C, potassium, and magnesium. Vitamin C is an antioxidant that supports the immune system and helps with wound healing. Potassium plays a crucial role in maintaining healthy blood pressure levels, and magnesium is important for bone health and nerve function.
- Recommended Portion Sizes: A typical serving size for grapefruits is half of a medium-sized fruit. It's essential to be mindful of portion sizes to manage blood sugar levels effectively. Monitoring blood sugar levels after consuming grapefruits can help individuals understand their body's response and make necessary adjustments to their meal plans.

Incorporating grapefruits into a diabetic diet can be done in various ways. Here are six different ideas to enjoy grapefruits as part of a diabetic-friendly diet:

1. Fresh Grapefruit: Simply enjoy a fresh grapefruit by cutting it in half and scooping out the segments. This is a refreshing and nutritious snack option.

2. Grapefruit Salad: Combine grapefruit segments with mixed greens, sliced almonds, and a light vinaigrette dressing for a refreshing and fiber-rich salad.

3. Grapefruit Smoothie: Blend grapefruit segments with low-fat yogurt, a handful of spinach, and a splash of almond milk for a nutritious and delicious smoothie.

4. Grilled Grapefruit: Cut a grapefruit in half, sprinkle with a touch of cinnamon and a drizzle of honey, and grill it for a few minutes. This warm and tangy treat can be enjoyed as a dessert or a snack.

5. Grapefruit Salsa: Dice grapefruit segments and combine them with diced tomatoes, onions, jalapenos, cilantro, and a squeeze of lime juice. This zesty salsa can be enjoyed with grilled chicken or fish.

6. Baked Grapefruit: Sprinkle grapefruit halves with a little brown sugar and cinnamon, then bake them until the sugar caramelizes. This warm and sweet treat can be enjoyed as a guilt-free dessert.

By incorporating grapefruits into a diabetic diet, individuals can enjoy a delicious and nutritious fruit that promotes better blood sugar control and overall health. Remember to monitor blood sugar levels and portion sizes to maintain optimal diabetes management.

B. Oranges

Oranges are a nutritious and delicious fruit that can be enjoyed as part of a diabetic-friendly diet. This topic provides a detailed description of oranges for diabetic health management, including its benefits.

Oranges have a low glycemic index; thus, they have little effect on blood sugar levels. This makes them a great choice for individuals with diabetes who need to monitor their blood sugar levels. The low glycemic index of oranges ensures that they do not cause a rapid spike in blood sugar levels, providing a steady release of energy.

In addition to being low in glycemic index, oranges are also a good source of carbohydrates. Carbohydrates are an essential macronutrient that provides energy to the body. The carbohydrates in oranges are digested and absorbed slowly, preventing sudden increases in blood sugar levels.

Oranges are also rich in dietary fiber, which is beneficial for individuals with diabetes. Fiber regulates blood sugar levels by decreasing the absorption of glucose into the circulation. It also improves intestinal health and prevents constipation.

When it comes to fat content, oranges are low in fat and contain no unhealthy saturated fats. This makes them a healthy choice for individuals with diabetes who need to manage their fat intake.

However, it's important to note that oranges are not a significant source of protein. Individuals with diabetes should ensure they are getting enough protein from other sources to support their overall health and wellbeing.

Oranges are packed with essential vitamins and minerals that are beneficial for individuals with diabetes. They are particularly rich in vitamin C, which is an antioxidant that helps boost the immune system and promote overall health. Oranges also contain folate, potassium, and calcium, which are important for various bodily functions.

For diabetic health management, it is recommended to consume one medium-sized orange as a serving. This portion size provides the necessary nutrients without causing a significant impact on blood sugar levels.

Incorporating oranges into a diabetic-friendly diet can be done in various ways. They can be enjoyed fresh as a snack or added to salads for a burst of citrus flavor. Oranges can also be juiced without added sugar to make a refreshing beverage. Additionally, oranges can be blended into smoothies with leafy greens like spinach or kale for a nutritious and satisfying drink. Grilling oranges with cinnamon and honey can create a warm treat, while making a salsa with oranges, tomatoes, onions, jalapenos, cilantro, and lime juice can add a tangy twist to meals.

It is important for individuals with diabetes to monitor their blood sugar levels and consult with healthcare professionals for personalized guidance on incorporating oranges into their diet.

C. Lemons

Lemons, a citrus fruit widely used for diabetic health management, offer numerous benefits due to their high content of vitamin C and other essential nutrients. Similar to oranges, lemons have a low glycemic index, making them a suitable choice for individuals with diabetes. This means that consuming lemons has a minimal impact on blood sugar levels.

One of the key advantages of lemons for diabetes management is their low carbohydrate content. Carbohydrates are the main nutrient that affects blood sugar levels, and lemons have a relatively low amount compared to other fruits. This makes lemons a favorable option for individuals who need to regulate their blood sugar levels.

In addition to being low in carbohydrates, lemons are also high in fiber. Fiber helps to regulate blood sugar levels by slowing carbohydrate breakdown and absorption. This helps prevent sudden spikes in blood sugar levels after a meal. Incorporating lemons into the diet can contribute to better blood sugar control and overall diabetes management.

Lemons also contain healthy fats, such as omega-3 fatty acids, which are beneficial for heart health. These fats have been shown to reduce inflammation and improve cholesterol levels, both of which are important for individuals with diabetes who are at a higher risk of heart disease.

Furthermore, lemons provide a good source of lean protein, vitamins, and minerals. Protein is essential for repairing and building tissues, and it can help keep you feeling full longer. Vitamins such as vitamin B6 and folate are important for various bodily functions, including energy metabolism and red blood cell production. Minerals like potassium and magnesium play a role in maintaining healthy blood pressure and promoting proper nerve and muscle function.

When incorporating lemons into the diet, it is important to be mindful of portion sizes. A recommended portion size is approximately 1 lemon, which weighs around 58 grams, or 1 tablespoon of lemon juice. This ensures that you are getting the benefits of lemons without consuming excessive amounts of carbohydrates or calories.

It is important to note that the information provided here is for informational purposes only and should not be considered as medical advice. It is always recommended to consult with a healthcare professional or a registered dietitian for personalized dietary recommendations tailored to your specific needs and health condition. They can provide you with guidance on how to incorporate lemons into your diet in a way that supports your diabetes management goals.

D. Limes

Limes are citrus fruits that are beneficial for diabetic health management. They are packed with essential nutrients and have a low glycemic index, making them a suitable choice for individuals with diabetes. Limes are rich in vitamin C, which helps boost the immune system and promote overall health. They also contain fiber, which aids in digestion and helps regulate blood sugar levels. Additionally, limes are a good source of potassium, a mineral that plays a vital role in maintaining heart health and blood pressure.

When it comes to managing diabetes, it is important to pay attention to the glycemic index of the foods we consume. The glycemic index measures how rapidly a certain item raises blood sugar levels. Limes have a low glycemic index, therefore they have little effect on blood sugar levels. This makes them an excellent alternative for anyone who need to manage their blood sugar levels.

In addition to their low glycemic index, limes are also low in carbohydrates. This is beneficial for individuals following a low-carb diet or those who need to monitor their carbohydrate intake. Limes can be incorporated into a variety of dishes and beverages without significantly affecting blood sugar levels.

One of the key benefits of limes for diabetic health management is their high vitamin C content. Vitamin C is a powerful antioxidant that helps protect cells from damage and boosts the immune system. For individuals with diabetes, maintaining a strong immune system is crucial for overall health and well-being.

Limes also contain dietary fiber, which is important for digestion and blood sugar regulation. Fiber helps to decrease the absorption of sugar into the circulation, reducing blood sugar rises. It also increases a sense of fullness, which aids with weight management.

Another nutrient found in limes is potassium. Potassium is essential for maintaining heart health and regulating blood pressure. Individuals with diabetes are at a higher risk of developing heart disease, so incorporating potassium-rich foods like limes into their diet can be beneficial.

It is important to note that limes are not a significant source of fat or protein. They are low in fat and do not contain unhealthy saturated fats. However, they do provide a good amount of vitamin C and potassium.

When consuming limes, it is recommended to do so in moderation as part of a balanced diet. One lime typically provides enough vitamin C for daily requirements. As with any dietary adjustment, it is always best to see a healthcare expert or a certified dietitian for individualized advice based on your specific health requirements and objectives.

In conclusion, limes are a beneficial fruit for individuals with diabetes. They have a low glycemic index, are low in carbohydrates, and contain essential nutrients like vitamin C and potassium. Incorporating limes into a balanced diet can support diabetic health management and overall well-being.

Berries

One of the key advantages of incorporating berries into a diabetic diet is their low glycemic index. The glycemic index calculates how rapidly a meal raises blood sugar levels. Berries have a low glycemic index, which means they cause a gradual and steady increase in blood sugar levels. This is particularly important for individuals with diabetes who need to manage their blood sugar levels effectively.

Berries have a low glycemic index and are high in dietary fiber. Fiber helps regulate blood sugar levels by decreasing glucose absorption into the circulation. Individuals with diabetes can benefit from eating berries since they help to regulate and stabilize blood sugar levels.

Berries also include antioxidants, such as anthocyanins, which have anti-inflammatory effects. Diabetes complications frequently include inflammation, which can cause a variety of health problems. Berries include antioxidants, which assist to decrease inflammation and protect against diabetic problems.

Furthermore, berries are a great source of vitamins and minerals that support overall health and well-being. They are particularly rich in vitamin C, which aids in boosting the immune system and promoting wound healing— both of which are important for individuals with diabetes. Berries also contain minerals like potassium and manganese, which play a role in maintaining healthy blood pressure and supporting bone health.

A. Blueberries

Blueberries are a type of small, round fruit that is known for its vibrant blue color. They are rich in antioxidants and have been found to have several health benefits, especially for diabetic health management. Blueberries have a low glycemic index, which means they have a minimal impact on blood sugar levels. This is particularly important for individuals with diabetes, as managing blood sugar levels is crucial for their overall health.

One of the key benefits of blueberries is their low carbohydrate content. Carbohydrates can significantly impact blood sugar levels, so choosing foods with a low carbohydrate content is essential for individuals with diabetes. Blueberries are also high in fiber, which further helps regulate blood sugar levels. Fiber slows down the absorption of glucose in the bloodstream, preventing spikes in blood sugar levels and promoting stable blood sugar control.

In addition to their low glycemic index and high fiber content, blueberries also contain healthy fats and lean protein. Healthy fats are important for maintaining overall health and well-being. They offer energy, promote cell development, and aid in the absorption of important vitamins. Lean protein, on the other hand, is critical for muscle development and repair.

Blueberries are good for both blood sugar control and overall wellness.

They are a good source of key vitamins and minerals, including vitamin C and vitamin K. Vitamin C is an antioxidant that supports immune function and helps protect against oxidative stress. Vitamin K is important for blood clotting and bone health. Blueberries also contain small amounts of vitamin E, vitamin B6, and folate, which are all essential for various bodily functions.

In terms of minerals, blueberries are rich in manganese, which plays a role in metabolism and bone health. They also contain small amounts of potassium and copper, which are important for maintaining healthy blood pressure and supporting the production of red blood cells, respectively.

When incorporating blueberries into a diabetic diet, it is important to consider portion sizes. A serving of blueberries is typically around 1 cup (148 grams). However, it is crucial to consult with a healthcare professional or a registered dietitian to determine the appropriate portion size based on individual dietary needs and goals.

In conclusion, blueberries are a nutritious fruit that can be a valuable addition to a diabetic diet. They have a low glycemic index, low carbohydrate content, and high fiber content, making them an excellent choice for managing blood sugar levels. Blueberries also provide essential vitamins and minerals, as well as healthy fats and lean protein. However, it is always recommended to consult with a healthcare professional or a registered dietitian for personalized dietary recommendations based on individual needs and goals.

B. Strawberries

Strawberries are a delicious and nutritious fruit that offer numerous benefits for diabetic health management. They are not only low in calories, but also have a low glycemic index, making them an excellent choice for individuals looking to regulate their blood sugar levels. The high fiber content found in strawberries further contributes to their positive impact on blood sugar control and digestion.

When it comes to nutritional value, strawberries are a powerhouse. In just 100 grams of strawberries, you can expect to find approximately 7 grams of carbohydrates. This information is very useful for people who need to closely control their carbohydrate consumption. Moreover, strawberries contain approximately 2 grams of fiber per 100 grams, which aids in maintaining stable blood sugar levels and promoting healthy digestion.

One of the standout features of strawberries is their negligible amount of healthy fats. This makes them an ideal choice for individuals who are conscious of their fat intake or are following a low-fat diet. Additionally, strawberries provide a modest amount of lean protein, with approximately 0.7 grams per 100 grams. While not a substantial source of protein, any amount helps to complete out a healthy diet.

In terms of essential vitamins and minerals, strawberries are a treasure trove. They are particularly rich in vitamin C, which is not only beneficial for overall health, but also plays a role in supporting a robust immune system. Additionally, strawberries contain important minerals, such as manganese and folate, which are essential for various bodily functions and contribute to overall wellbeing.

To enjoy the benefits of strawberries while managing diabetes or any other medical condition, it is always advisable to consult with a healthcare professional or a registered dietitian. They can provide personalized guidance and help incorporate strawberries into a well-balanced diet that meets individual needs.

In conclusion, strawberries are a versatile and nutritious fruit that can greatly contribute to diabetic health management. With their low glycemic index, high fiber content, and abundance of essential vitamins and minerals, they offer a multitude of benefits. Whether enjoyed as a snack, added to salads, or used in smoothies, strawberries are a delicious and healthy addition to any diet. So go ahead and savor the sweetness of strawberries while reaping their numerous health benefits.

Tomatoes

Tomatoes are not only delicious, but also a valuable addition to a diabetic diet. Incorporating tomatoes into meals can provide numerous nutritional benefits and help manage blood sugar levels. In this comprehensive discussion, we will explore the various ways tomatoes can be included in a diabetic diet, their impact on blood sugar levels, and the overall benefits they offer.

Tomatoes are a rich source of essential nutrients, including vitamins A, C, and E, as well as potassium and fiber. These nutrients are vital for maintaining overall health, especially for individuals with diabetes. Tomatoes' high fiber content can help manage blood sugar levels by decreasing glucose absorption into the circulation. This can minimize unexpected rises in blood sugar levels, making tomatoes a great choice for diabetics.

Moreover, tomatoes are low in calories and have a low glycemic index, which means they have a minimal impact on blood sugar levels. This makes them an appropriate choice for people who want to maintain their weight while also controlling their blood sugar levels. Incorporating tomatoes into a diabetic diet can help individuals feel fuller for longer, reducing the temptation to snack on unhealthy foods.

There are various ways to include tomatoes in meals while keeping them diabetes-friendly. One simple method is to add sliced tomatoes to salads or sandwiches. This adds a burst of flavor and nutrients without significantly affecting blood sugar levels. Another option is to use tomatoes as a base for homemade sauces or salsas. By making these sauces from scratch, individuals can control the amount of added sugar and other ingredients, making them a healthier choice.

For those who enjoy cooking, incorporating tomatoes into main dishes can be both delicious and nutritious. One idea is to stuff tomatoes with a mixture of lean protein, such as ground turkey or tofu, and vegetables. This creates a satisfying and balanced meal that is low in carbohydrates and high in nutrients. Another option is to roast tomatoes with a drizzle of olive oil and a sprinkle of herbs. This enhances their natural sweetness and can be served as a side dish or added to pasta dishes for extra flavor.

In addition to their culinary uses, tomatoes can also be enjoyed in the form of fresh juices or smoothies. By blending ripe tomatoes with other fruits and vegetables, individuals can create refreshing and nutrient-packed beverages. However, it is essential to be mindful of portion sizes and the overall carbohydrate content when consuming tomato-based drinks to avoid any adverse effects on blood sugar levels.

While the nutritional benefits and culinary versatility of tomatoes make them an excellent choice for a diabetic diet, it is crucial to consult with a healthcare professional or a registered dietitian before making any significant changes to your diet. They can provide personalized guidance and help you incorporate tomatoes and other foods into your meal plan in a way that best suits your individual needs and health goals.

A. Tomatoes

Tomatoes are a versatile and nutritious food that can be easily incorporated into a diabetic diet. They offer numerous health benefits and are particularly beneficial for individuals looking to manage their blood sugar levels.

One of the key nutritional aspects of tomatoes is their low glycemic index. This implies they have little effect on blood sugar levels when ingested. Diabetic individuals can enjoy tomatoes without worrying about significant spikes in their blood sugar levels.

In addition to being low in carbohydrates, tomatoes are also a good source of dietary fiber. Fiber is important for regulating blood sugar levels and promoting digestive health. It delays the absorption of sugar into the circulation, reducing rapid blood sugar fluctuations. Incorporating tomatoes into your meals can help you maintain stable blood sugar levels throughout the day.

Tomatoes are also low in fat and contain mainly healthy fats, such as omega-3 fatty acids. This makes them a great choice for individuals looking to maintain a healthy weight and reduce the risk of heart disease, which is often associated with diabetes.

While tomatoes are not a significant source of protein, they do contribute a small amount to the overall protein intake. Protein is essential for tissue growth and repair, as well as immune system function. In terms of vitamins and minerals, tomatoes are rich in essential nutrients. They are an excellent source of vitamin C, which is known for its immune-boosting properties. Tomatoes also contain vitamin A, which is important for maintaining healthy vision and supporting the immune system. Additionally, tomatoes are a good source of potassium, which plays a crucial role in maintaining healthy blood pressure levels.

When incorporating tomatoes into your diabetic diet, it is important to be mindful of portion sizes. A recommended portion size of tomatoes for diabetic individuals is about 1 cup or 150 grams. This ensures that you are getting the health benefits of tomatoes without consuming excessive carbohydrates or calories.

In conclusion, tomatoes are a nutritious and diabetes-friendly food that can be enjoyed in various forms. Whether fresh, canned, or cooked, tomatoes can be added to salads, sandwiches, sauces, and breakfast dishes. By including tomatoes in your meals, you can reap their health benefits while adding flavor and variety to your diet. Remember to consult with a healthcare professional for personalized dietary recommendations for diabetes management.

CHAPTER 9: FISH HIGH IN OMEGA-3 FATTY ACIDS

One of the key advantages of omega-3 fatty acids is their ability to reduce inflammation in the body. Inflammation is a common issue in diabetes, and it can contribute to various complications. By incorporating fish high in omega-3 fatty acids into their diet, individuals with diabetes can help alleviate inflammation and reduce the risk of related complications.

Another important benefit of omega-3 fatty acids for diabetic patients is their ability to improve insulin sensitivity. Insulin resistance is a hallmark of diabetes, and it can lead to elevated blood sugar levels. Studies have shown that omega-3 fatty acids can enhance insulin sensitivity, allowing for better blood sugar control. This can help diabetics better control their condition.

Furthermore, fish high in omega-3 fatty acids can help lower the risk of heart disease in diabetic patients. Heart disease is a major concern for individuals with diabetes, as they are at a higher risk of developing cardiovascular complications. Omega-3 fatty acids have been shown to reduce triglyceride levels, decrease blood pressure, and improve overall heart health. By including fish rich in omega-3 fatty acids in their diet, individuals with diabetes can take proactive steps towards protecting their cardiovascular health.

When it comes to the recommended intake of omega-3 fatty acids, the American Heart Association suggests consuming at least two servings of fatty fish per week. Salmon, mackerel, sardines, and trout are all good sources of omega-3 fatty acids. These fish are not only delicious but also provide a significant amount of omega-3 fatty acids.

Salmon

Salmon is a highly beneficial food for individuals managing diabetes. It offers a range of health benefits and is an excellent source of essential nutrients. Here are some key points about salmon's nutritional profile:

• Glycemic index: Salmon has a low glycemic index, which means it does not cause a rapid increase in blood sugar levels. This makes it a suitable choice for individuals with diabetes who need to manage their blood sugar levels.

• Carbohydrate content: Salmon is low in carbohydrates, making it an ideal option for diabetic individuals who need to control their carbohydrate intake. This can help avoid blood sugar increases.

- Fiber content: Salmon is a good source of dietary fiber. Fiber helps regulate blood sugar levels and promotes intestinal health. Including salmon in the diet can help individuals with diabetes maintain stable blood sugar levels.
- Healthy fats: Salmon is rich in omega-3 fatty acids, which have been shown to have numerous health benefits. These healthy fats can reduce inflammation, improve insulin sensitivity, and lower the risk of heart disease in individuals with diabetes. Omega-3 fatty acids are essential for managing diabetes and optimizing overall health.
- Lean protein content: Salmon is a lean source of protein. Protein is important for building and repairing tissues, as well as maintaining muscle mass. Including salmon in the diet can help individuals with diabetes meet their protein needs without consuming excessive amounts of fat.
- Key vitamins and minerals: Salmon is packed with essential vitamins and minerals that are beneficial for individuals with diabetes. It contains high levels of vitamin D, which is essential for bone health and immunological function. Salmon also contains vitamin B12, selenium, and potassium, all of which are essential for general health.
- Recommended portion sizes: The American Diabetes Association recommends consuming 3-4 ounces of cooked salmon per serving. This is approximately the size of a deck of cards. Following these portion sizes can help individuals with diabetes manage their calorie and nutrient intake effectively.

Herring

Herrings are a type of fish that can be highly beneficial for individuals managing diabetes. Similar to salmon, herrings have a low glycemic index, which means they have a minimal impact on blood sugar levels. This makes herrings an excellent choice for controlling blood sugar levels in individuals with diabetes.

One of the key advantages of herrings is their low carbohydrate content. They are naturally low in carbohydrates, making them suitable for individuals who need to monitor their carbohydrate intake to manage their diabetes effectively. With their negligible carbohydrate content, herrings can be included in a diabetes-friendly diet without causing significant spikes in blood sugar levels.

Herrings are also rich in dietary fiber, which is essential for regulating blood sugar levels. Fiber reduces glucose absorption in the circulation, which helps to minimize blood sugar rises. Individuals with diabetes who incorporate herrings into their diet might benefit from the high fiber content and better regulate their blood sugar levels.

Another notable aspect of herrings is their healthy fat content, particularly omega-3 fatty acids. These fatty acids have been demonstrated to lower inflammation in the body while also improving insulin sensitivity. By consuming herrings, individuals with diabetes can potentially reduce the risk of complications associated with chronic inflammation and improve their body's response to insulin.

In addition to being a good source of healthy fats, herrings are also rich in lean protein. Protein is necessary for the body's tissue formation and repair. Including herrings in the diet can help diabetics satisfy their protein requirements without adding too much saturated fat or cholesterol.

Herrings are packed with essential vitamins and minerals that are beneficial for overall health and diabetes management. They are a good source of vitamin D, which plays a crucial role in bone health and immune function. Vitamin B12, selenium, phosphorus, and potassium are also found in herrings, contributing to various bodily functions and supporting overall well-being.

To incorporate herrings into a diabetes-friendly diet, it is recommended to consume 2-3 servings per week, with each serving being about 3-4 ounces. This portion size ensures a balanced intake of essential nutrients without exceeding calorie or fat limits.

In summary, herrings are a highly beneficial food for individuals managing diabetes. With their low glycemic index, negligible carbohydrate content, high fiber content, healthy fats, lean protein, and essential vitamins and minerals, herrings can support blood sugar control and overall health in individuals with diabetes. By including herrings in their diet, individuals with diabetes can optimize their health and effectively manage their condition.

Sardines

Sardines are a type of small, oily fish that are highly beneficial for diabetic health management. They are packed with essential nutrients and offer numerous health benefits. Incorporating sardines into a diabetic diet can help regulate blood sugar levels, promote heart health, and support overall well-being.

Sardines have a low glycemic index, which means they have a minimal impact on blood sugar levels. This makes them an ideal choice for individuals managing diabetes. Unlike foods with high glycemic index, sardines do not cause rapid spikes in blood sugar levels, helping to maintain stable blood sugar levels throughout the day.

One of the key advantages of sardines for diabetics is their low carbohydrate content. Carbohydrates are the main nutrient that affects blood sugar levels, and sardines contain very few carbohydrates. This makes them a suitable option for individuals who need to control their carbohydrate intake to manage their blood sugar levels effectively.

Sardines are also rich in dietary fiber. Fiber is essential for digestion and helps regulate blood sugar levels. It inhibits glucose absorption into the circulation, which prevents blood sugar rises. Sardines in your diabetic diet plan can help you achieve your daily fiber needs while also supporting good digestion.

In addition to being low in carbohydrates and high in fiber, sardines are rich in healthy fats. They are an excellent source of omega-3 fatty acids, which have been shown to have numerous health benefits. Omega-3 fatty acids help reduce inflammation, improve heart health, and support brain function. Including sardines in your diet can help lower the risk of heart disease, a common complication of diabetes.

Sardines are also a great source of lean protein. Protein is essential for muscle growth and repair, and it helps keep you feeling full and satisfied after meals. Sardines can help you achieve your protein needs without adding too many calories or bad fats to your diabetic diet.

In terms of vitamins and minerals, sardines are packed with essential nutrients. They contain high levels of vitamin B12, which is essential for nerve function and red blood cell synthesis. Sardines also provide vitamin D, calcium, and selenium, which are essential for bone health, immune function, and antioxidant protection.

When incorporating sardines into your diabetic meal plan, it is recommended to consume 2-3 servings per week. A typical serving size of sardines is 3.5 ounces (100 grams), which provides a good balance of nutrients without excessive calorie intake. You can enjoy sardines in various ways, such as grilled, baked, or added to salads or pasta dishes.

By including sardines in your diabetic meal plan, you can enjoy their delicious taste while reaping the numerous health benefits they offer. They are a nutritious and versatile food option that can support your diabetes management and overall well-being.

CHAPTER 10: ADVANCED DIABETIC MENU PLANNING

The guide is designed to cater to a varied audience, ranging from high school students to college-educated individuals. It offers step-by-step instructions and practical examples to simplify the process of meal planning for individuals with diabetes.

One of the key areas covered in this topic is portion control. It emphasizes the importance of understanding portion sizes and how they can impact blood sugar levels. The content provides clear guidelines on how to measure and control portion sizes to maintain stable glucose levels.

Carbohydrate counting is another crucial aspect addressed in this topic. It explains how carbohydrates affect blood sugar levels and provides strategies for accurately counting carbohydrates in meals. The guide also offers practical tips on incorporating a variety of carbohydrates into meal plans while still maintaining blood sugar control.

Choosing the right ingredients is essential for creating balanced and nutritious meals for individuals with diabetes. This topic provides guidance on identifying suitable ingredients that are low in added sugars, saturated fats, and sodium. It also highlights the significance of including a range of fruits, vegetables, whole grains, lean meats, and healthy fats in your meal plan.

Meal Planning

Meal planning is a crucial aspect of managing diabetes effectively. It involves creating balanced and diabetic-friendly meal plans that help regulate blood sugar levels and maintain overall health. In this section, we will provide step-by-step strategies for planning diabetic-friendly meals.

1. Portion Control

Portion control plays a significant role in managing diabetes. It involves managing the quantity of food consumed to maintain a healthy weight and control blood sugar levels. Understanding portion sizes and using measuring tools can help individuals with diabetes make informed choices about their meals.

2. Carbohydrate Counting

Carbohydrate counting is a method used by individuals with diabetes to manage their carbohydrate intake. It involves monitoring the number of carbohydrates consumed in each meal to regulate blood sugar levels. This technique helps individuals make appropriate food choices and maintain stable glucose levels throughout the day.

3. Selecting Appropriate Ingredients

Choosing the right ingredients is essential for creating diabetic-friendly meals. Opting for whole grains, lean proteins, and healthy fats can help control blood sugar levels and improve overall health. Incorporating a variety of fruits and vegetables provides essential nutrients while adding flavor and texture to meals.

4. Meal Planning Tools

Utilizing meal planning tools can simplify the process of creating diabetic-friendly meal plans. These tools may include meal planning apps, recipe websites, or even simple pen and paper. Planning meals in advance and creating a shopping list can help individuals stay organized and make healthier choices while grocery shopping.

5. Balanced Meal Composition

A balanced meal for individuals with diabetes typically consists of a combination of carbohydrates, proteins, and fats. Including high-fiber carbohydrates, such as whole grains and legumes, can help regulate blood sugar levels. Adding lean proteins, such as poultry, fish, or tofu, aids in maintaining satiety and managing weight. Healthy fats, like avocados or nuts, provide essential nutrients and contribute to a well-rounded meal.

6. Meal Prepping

Meal prepping can be a valuable strategy for individuals with diabetes. It entails prepping meals or ingredients in advance to save time and make better choices during the week. By dedicating a specific day to meal preparation, individuals can have ready-to-eat meals or pre-cut ingredients available, making it easier to stick to their diabetic meal plan.

7. Seeking Professional Guidance

It is important for individuals with diabetes to consult with a registered dietitian or healthcare professional for personalized meal planning guidance. These experts can provide tailored recommendations based on individual needs, preferences, and health goals. They can also address any concerns or questions related to diabetes management and meal planning.

By following these step-by-step strategies, individuals with diabetes can create personalized and diabetic-friendly meal plans. These plans will not only help regulate blood sugar levels but also contribute to overall health and well-being. Remember, meal planning is a continuous process that requires experimentation and adjustment to find the best approach for each individual.

CHAPTER 11: BUSTING MYTHS ABOUT DIABETIC DIETS

In this section, we will address and correct some common myths surrounding diabetic diets. It is important to clarify these misconceptions and provide accurate information to help individuals manage their diabetes effectively.

Myth 1: People with diabetes cannot eat sugar at all.

Fact: While it is true that individuals with diabetes need to monitor their sugar intake, it does not mean they have to completely eliminate sugar from their diet. The key is to consume sugar in moderation and be mindful of portion sizes. It is recommended to choose natural sources of sugar, such as fruits, and avoid processed foods with added sugars.

Myth 2: Diabetic diets are restrictive and boring.

Fact: A diabetic diet does not have to be boring or restrictive. It is all about making healthy food choices and incorporating a variety of nutritious foods. There are plenty of delicious options available, including whole grains, lean proteins, fruits, vegetables, and low-fat dairy products. With proper planning and creativity, individuals with diabetes can enjoy flavorful meals while managing their blood sugar levels.

Myth 3: Artificial sweeteners are a safe alternative to sugar.

Fact: Artificial sweeteners may seem like a good option for individuals with diabetes, but it is important to use them in moderation. Some studies suggest that excessive consumption of artificial sweeteners may have negative effects on metabolic health. It is best to consult with a healthcare professional to determine the appropriate use of artificial sweeteners in one's diet.

Myth 4: Carbohydrates should be completely avoided in a diabetic diet.

Fact: Carbohydrates are an essential nutrient and should not be completely eliminated from a diabetic diet. However, it is critical to select complex carbs that are high in fiber and have a low glycemic load. These include whole grains, legumes, and vegetables. Monitoring portion sizes and spreading carbohydrate intake throughout the day can help regulate blood sugar levels more efficiently.

Myth 5: Only overweight individuals develop diabetes.

Fact: While being overweight or obese can increase the risk of developing type 2 diabetes, it is not the sole factor. Genetics, lifestyle choices, and other medical conditions can also contribute to the development of diabetes. It is important to focus on overall health and make positive lifestyle changes, regardless of weight, to prevent or manage diabetes.

Myth 6: Insulin is a cure for diabetes.

Fact: Insulin is not a cure for diabetes but rather a vital treatment option for individuals with type 1 diabetes or advanced type 2 diabetes. It helps to manage blood sugar levels, but it does not treat the underlying causes of diabetes. Lifestyle changes, such as a nutritious diet, frequent exercise, and medication management, are essential for long-term diabetes control.

By refuting these beliefs and giving correct information, we hope to empower people with diabetes to make educated dietary choices. It is important to consult with healthcare professionals and registered dietitians to develop personalized meal plans that cater to individual needs and goals. With the right knowledge and support, individuals with diabetes can lead a healthy and fulfilling life.

Fact-Based Information

Living with diabetes can be challenging, but armed with fact-based information and a solid understanding of diabetes management, you can take control of your health and well-being. In this comprehensive guide, we will delve into the key aspects of diabetes diets, address common misconceptions, and provide base dietary advice based on scientific research and best practices. Whether you have recently been diagnosed or have been managing diabetes for years, this guide will empower you with the knowledge you need to make informed decisions about your health.

Understanding Diabetes

Before we dive into the specifics of diabetes management, let's start by understanding the condition itself. Diabetes is a chronic metabolic condition marked by elevated blood sugar levels. It happens when the body either generates insufficient insulin (a hormone that controls blood sugar) or is unable to adequately utilize the insulin it produces. There are different types of diabetes, including type 1, type 2, and gestational diabetes. Each type requires a tailored approach to management, and consulting with a healthcare professional is crucial to developing a personalized plan.

Common Misconceptions

There are numerous misconceptions surrounding diabetes, and it's important to address them to dispel any confusion. One common misconception is that diabetes is caused solely by consuming too much sugar. While excessive sugar intake can contribute to the development of type 2 diabetes, it is not the sole cause. Other factors, such as genetics, lifestyle choices, and obesity, also play a significant role. Another misconception is that people with diabetes must follow a strict and bland diet. In reality, a balanced and varied diet can be enjoyed while effectively managing blood sugar levels.

Base Dietary Advice

Now that we have explored the key aspects of diabetes diets, let's focus on some base dietary advice that can benefit individuals with diabetes:

1. Emphasize Whole Foods: Incorporate a variety of whole, unprocessed foods into your diet, such as fruits, vegetables, whole grains, lean proteins, and healthy fats. These foods are rich in nutrients and fiber, which can help regulate blood sugar levels and promote overall health.

2. Limit Sugary and Processed Foods: Minimize your consumption of sugary beverages, desserts, and processed snacks. These foods can cause rapid spikes in blood sugar and provide little nutritional value.

3. Stay Hydrated: Drinking an adequate amount of water is essential for everyone, including individuals with diabetes. Water helps maintain hydration, supports kidney function, and aids in digestion.

4. Regular Physical Activity: Engaging in regular physical activity can improve insulin sensitivity, help maintain a healthy weight, and promote overall well-being. Consult with your healthcare team to develop an exercise plan suitable for your individual needs.

CHAPTER 12: ADDITIONAL RESOURCES

Within this chapter, you will find a comprehensive list of relevant sources that can provide additional insights or assistance. These resources encompass a variety of mediums, including books, articles, websites, and other materials. Each resource has been carefully selected to enhance the reader's understanding and provide them with additional avenues for exploration.

Whether you are a high school student looking to delve deeper into the topic or a college-educated individual seeking more advanced resources, this chapter has something to offer for everyone. By utilizing the resources mentioned here, you can broaden your knowledge and gain a more comprehensive understanding of the subject matter.

Reading List

A reading list is an invaluable tool for individuals seeking to delve deeper into a particular topic. It serves as a curated collection of recommended resources that can enhance one's understanding and provide a comprehensive exploration of a subject matter. In the case of this reading list, we will be focusing on books, articles, and websites that offer in-depth exploration of the topic at hand.

Books:

1. "The Power of Habit: Why We Do What We Do in Life and Business" by Charles Duhigg: This book delves into the science behind habits and explores how they shape our lives, both personally and professionally. Duhigg provides fascinating insights and practical strategies for harnessing the power of habit to achieve success.

2. "Quiet: The Power of Introverts in a World That Can't Stop Talking" by Susan Cain: Cain's book challenges the notion that extroversion is the ideal personality trait and celebrates the strengths and contributions of introverts. Through extensive research and compelling anecdotes, she highlights the power of introversion in various aspects of life.

3. "Sapiens: A Brief History of Humankind" by Yuval Noah Harari: Harari takes readers on a captivating journey through the history of humankind, exploring the key milestones that have shaped our species. From the emergence of Homo sapiens to the present day, this book offers a thought-provoking perspective on our collective story.

Articles:

1. "The Science of Happiness" by Sonja Lyubomirsky: In this article, Lyubomirsky explores the research behind happiness and offers practical strategies for cultivating a more joyful and fulfilling life. Drawing from positive psychology, she provides evidence-based insights that can positively impact our well-being.

2. "The Rise of Artificial Intelligence: Implications and Ethics" by Nick Bostrom: Bostrom's article delves into the world of artificial intelligence, examining its potential implications and ethical considerations. He raises thought-provoking questions about the future of AI and its impact on society.

Websites:

3. TED Talks (www.ted.com): TED Talks feature a wide range of captivating speakers who share their insights and expertise on various topics. The website offers a vast collection of talks that can provide valuable perspectives and inspire further exploration.

4. Stanford Encyclopedia of Philosophy (plato.stanford.edu): This online resource provides comprehensive and authoritative articles on a wide range of philosophical topics. It serves as an excellent reference for those seeking in-depth exploration and understanding of philosophical concepts.

By incorporating these recommended resources into your reading list, you can embark on a journey of in-depth exploration and gain a deeper understanding of the topic at hand. Whether you prefer delving into books, exploring thought-provoking articles, or immersing yourself in engaging websites, this reading list offers a diverse range of resources to satisfy your thirst for knowledge. Happy reading!

Support Networks

Living with diabetes can be a challenging journey, but fortunately, there are various support networks available to help individuals navigate this condition and improve their overall well-being. In this comprehensive discussion, we will explore the role and benefits of support groups, online communities, and diabetic education resources in managing diabetes. We will also provide guidance on how to access these valuable networks.

Support groups play a crucial role in providing emotional and practical support to individuals with diabetes. These groups bring together people who share similar experiences, allowing them to connect, share advice, and offer encouragement. By participating in support groups, individuals can gain a sense of belonging and find solace in knowing that they are not alone in their journey. Additionally, support groups provide a platform for learning from others' experiences, which can help individuals make more informed decisions about their own diabetes management.

To access support groups, individuals can start by reaching out to local healthcare providers, such as hospitals or community health centers, as they often facilitate these groups. Diabetes clinics and organizations dedicated to diabetes management are also excellent resources for finding support groups in your area. Online directories and social media platforms can also provide information about virtual support groups that individuals can join from the comfort of their own homes.

In today's digital age, online communities have become a valuable source of support for individuals living with diabetes. These communities offer a platform for individuals to connect with others, share their experiences, seek advice, and find encouragement. Online communities provide a sense of anonymity, allowing individuals to openly discuss their concerns and challenges without fear of judgment. Moreover, the 24/7 accessibility of online communities ensures that individuals can find support whenever they need it.

To join online communities, individuals can explore diabetes-specific websites, forums, and social media groups. These platforms often have dedicated sections or groups for diabetes-related discussions. By actively participating in these online communities, individuals can build connections, gain valuable insights, and receive support from a diverse range of perspectives.

In addition to support groups and online communities, diabetic education resources play a vital role in empowering individuals to manage their diabetes effectively. These resources provide valuable information on various aspects of diabetes, including self-care, medication management, nutrition, exercise, and coping strategies. By educating themselves about diabetes, individuals can make informed decisions and take proactive steps towards better managing their condition.

Accessing diabetic education resources is relatively easy, as they are widely available both online and offline. Local healthcare providers, such as hospitals and clinics, often offer diabetes education programs and workshops. Diabetes associations and organizations also provide comprehensive resources, including brochures, pamphlets, and online materials. Online platforms, such as reputable websites and mobile applications, offer a wealth of information, interactive tools, and educational videos to support individuals in their diabetes management journey.

By actively engaging with these networks, individuals can find comfort, gain knowledge, and develop strategies to effectively manage their condition. Remember, you are not alone in your journey with diabetes— there are support networks waiting to assist you every step of the way.

CHAPTER 13: NAVIGATING FOOD LABELS

To navigate food labels effectively, there are several key points to consider:

1. Serving Size: Understanding the serving size is essential, as all the information on the label is based on this amount. It is important to compare the serving size to the portion you actually consume. Calories: The calorie count per serving is listed on the label. This information helps you manage your calorie intake and make healthier choices.

2. Nutrients: The label provides information on various nutrients, including fats, carbohydrates, and proteins. It is important to pay attention to the types and amounts of these nutrients to maintain a balanced diet.

3. % Daily Value: The % Daily Value (%DV) indicates how much of a specific nutrient one serving provides in relation to the recommended daily intake. It helps you determine if a food item is high or low in a particular nutrient.

4. Ingredients: The ingredients list is an important section of the label. It lists all the components of the product in descending order by weight. This can help you identify any allergens or ingredients you may want to avoid.

5. Additional Information: Some food labels may provide additional information, such as allergen warnings, health claims, or certifications. It is important to be aware of these details if they apply to your dietary needs or preferences.

Decoding Nutritional Information

Understanding the nutritional content of the food we consume is essential for maintaining a healthy lifestyle. Food labels provide valuable information that can help us make informed choices about what we eat. In this comprehensive guide, we will explore the key aspects of decoding nutritional information, including serving sizes, total carbohydrates, sugars, and fiber. By the end, you will have the knowledge and tools to navigate food labels confidently and make healthier food choices.

Serving Sizes: The Foundation of Nutritional Information

Serving sizes play a crucial role in understanding the nutritional content of a food product. They provide a standardized measure of the quantity of food the label refers to when presenting its nutritional information. It is important to note that serving sizes can vary between products, so it's essential to compare them when evaluating different foods. By paying attention to serving sizes, you can accurately assess the nutritional value of the food you consume.

Total Carbohydrates: Unveiling the Energy Providers

Total carbohydrates represent the sum of all the different types of carbohydrates present in a food item, including sugars, fiber, and complex carbohydrates. Carbohydrates are a primary source of energy for our bodies, but not all carbohydrates are created equal. It is crucial to distinguish between simple sugars and complex carbohydrates.

Identifying Sugars: Differentiating Between Natural and Added Sugars

Sugars can occur naturally in foods, such as fruits and dairy products, or they can be added during processing. It is important to be aware of the distinction between natural and added sugars. Natural sugars, like those found in fruits, provide essential nutrients along with their sweetness. Added sugars, on the other hand, contribute empty calories without any nutritional value. To identify added sugars, look for ingredients such as corn syrup, high-fructose corn syrup, sucrose, or any word ending in "-ose" on the food label.

The Role of Fiber: A Key Component of a Healthy Diet

Fiber is an essential nutrient that aids in digestion and promotes overall gut health. It also helps regulate blood sugar levels and contributes to a feeling of fullness after a meal. When decoding nutritional information, look for the fiber content on the food label. Foods rich in fiber, such as whole grains, fruits, vegetables, and legumes, are excellent choices for a balanced diet.

Putting It All Together: Making Informed Food Choices

Now that you understand the technical aspects of decoding nutritional information, let's explore how to use this knowledge to make healthier food choices. Here are some tips and examples to guide you:

1. Pay attention to serving sizes: Compare the serving sizes of different products to ensure you are making accurate nutritional comparisons.

2. Choose foods with lower total carbohydrates: Opt for foods that are lower in total carbohydrates, especially if you are managing your blood sugar levels or following a low-carb diet.

3. Limit added sugars: Avoid foods with high amounts of added sugars. Instead, satisfy your sweet tooth with naturally sweetened options like fresh fruits.

4. Increase fiber intake: Select foods that are high in fiber to promote a healthy digestive system and maintain a feeling of fullness. Incorporate whole grains, fruits, vegetables, and legumes into your meals and snacks.

5. Be mindful of hidden sugars: Some processed foods, condiments, and beverages can contain significant amounts of hidden sugars. Read food labels carefully to identify and limit your intake of added sugars.

By following these tips and using the information provided on food labels, you can make informed choices that support a healthier lifestyle. Remember, decoding nutritional information is an ongoing process, and with practice, it will become second nature. Start today and embark on a journey towards a healthier, more balanced diet.

Identifying Hidden Sugars

Understanding the nutritional information on food labels is crucial for making informed choices about the foods we consume. This includes paying attention to serving sizes, calorie counts, total carbohydrates, sugars, fiber content, % Daily Value, and ingredients. By deciphering this information, individuals can make healthier choices that align with their dietary needs and goals.

One important aspect of reading food labels is identifying hidden sugars. Many processed foods contain added sugars, which can contribute to weight gain, increase the risk of chronic diseases, and negatively impact overall health. However, these added sugars can be disguised under different names in the ingredient list, making them difficult to spot.

To identify hidden sugars, it is essential to familiarize yourself with the various names that sugar can be listed as on food labels. Some common names for added sugars include sucrose, glucose, fructose, corn syrup, high fructose corn syrup, maltose, dextrose, and molasses. By recognizing these names, you can quickly identify if a product contains added sugars.

In addition to being aware of the different names for sugar, it is also important to pay attention to the placement of sugar in the ingredient list. Ingredients are listed in descending order by weight, so if sugar is listed as one of the first few ingredients, it indicates that the product likely contains a significant amount of added sugars. Conversely, if sugar is listed towards the end of the ingredient list, it suggests that the product contains a lower amount of added sugars.

Another technique to identify hidden sugars is to look for ingredients that end in "-ose." These are often sugars or substances that are converted into sugars in the body. Examples include maltose, sucrose, and dextrose. By recognizing these ingredients, you can be more aware of the sugar content in the product.

It is also important to be mindful of other unhealthy additives that may be present in processed foods. These include artificial sweeteners, preservatives, and artificial flavors or colors. Reading the ingredient list can help you identify these additives and make healthier choices by opting for products with fewer artificial ingredients.

By becoming proficient in identifying hidden sugars and unhealthy additives in ingredient lists, you can make more informed choices about the foods you consume. This knowledge empowers you to select products that align with your dietary needs and goals, ultimately contributing to a healthier diet and lifestyle.

Understanding Health Claims

Health claims are statements made on food packaging that describe the potential health benefits of consuming a particular product. These claims are regulated by government agencies to ensure accuracy and prevent misleading information. For individuals following a diabetic diet, it is crucial to understand and evaluate health claims to make informed choices about their food consumption.

Evaluating Health Claims

When assessing health claims on food packaging, there are several steps that can help individuals determine their relevance and accuracy. Firstly, it is important to read the entire claim and not just focus on the highlighted keywords. This will provide a better understanding of the context and potential limitations of the claim.

Next, individuals should consider the source of the claim. Is it backed by scientific research or is it merely a marketing tactic? Looking for credible sources such as reputable research institutions or health organizations can help validate the claim's reliability.

Furthermore, it is essential to examine the wording used in the claim. Claims that use terms like "may," "might," or "could" indicate a weaker level of evidence compared to claims that use stronger language such as "proven" or "supported by scientific research."

Importance for a Diabetic Diet

Understanding health claims is particularly important for individuals following a diabetic diet. These individuals need to carefully monitor their blood sugar levels and manage their carbohydrate intake. Health claims can provide valuable information about the nutritional content of a product and its potential impact on blood sugar levels.

By evaluating health claims, individuals can identify products that are low in added sugars, artificial sweeteners, and unhealthy additives. This knowledge allows them to make informed choices and select foods that align with their dietary needs and goals.

Examples of Relevant Health Claims

There are several health claims that are particularly relevant to managing diabetes. Claims such as "low sugar," "sugar-free," or "no added sugars" indicate that the product contains minimal or no added sugars, making it a suitable option for individuals with diabetes.

Claims related to low glycemic index (GI) can also be beneficial for individuals following a diabetic diet. Foods with a low GI value have a slower impact on blood sugar levels, helping to maintain stable glucose levels.

Additionally, claims related to high fiber content or whole grains can be advantageous for individuals with diabetes. These foods can help regulate blood sugar levels and promote better glycemic control.

In conclusion, understanding health claims is essential for individuals following a diabetic diet. By evaluating these claims, individuals can make informed choices about the foods they consume, ensuring that they align with their dietary needs and goals. Being proficient in identifying hidden sugars and unhealthy additives can contribute to a healthier diet and lifestyle for individuals managing diabetes.

Making Smart Choices

Living with diabetes requires careful consideration when it comes to making food choices. By analyzing food labels, individuals can make informed decisions about what they consume, ensuring that their meals align with their dietary needs. In this comprehensive guide, we will explore the technical aspects of selecting diabetic-friendly options based on food label analysis. By following the proper format in generating reviews, we will provide detailed, accurate, and informative information that will empower individuals to make smart choices for their health.

Understanding Food Labels

Before diving into the specifics of analyzing food labels, it is essential to understand the key components. Food labels provide vital information about the nutritional content of a product, including serving size, calories, macronutrients, and ingredients. By carefully examining these details, individuals can gain insights into the potential impact a particular food may have on their blood sugar levels.

Analyzing Carbohydrates

Carbohydrates play a significant role in managing diabetes, as they directly affect blood sugar levels. When analyzing food labels, it is crucial to pay attention to the total carbohydrates listed per serving. Additionally, individuals should look for the breakdown of carbohydrates into sugars and dietary fiber. Diabetic-friendly options typically have a lower sugar content and a higher fiber content, as fiber helps slow down the absorption of sugar into the bloodstream.

Evaluating Fat Content

While fat does not directly impact blood sugar levels, it is still important to consider when selecting diabetic-friendly options. Opting for foods that are low in saturated and trans fats can help promote heart health, which is often a concern for individuals with diabetes. Reading food labels can provide insights into the types and amounts of fat present in a product, allowing individuals to make choices that align with their dietary goals.

Considering Sodium Levels

Monitoring sodium intake is essential for managing diabetes, as high sodium levels can lead to increased blood pressure and other health complications. When analyzing food labels, individuals should pay attention to the sodium content per serving. Choosing options that are lower in sodium can help individuals maintain a balanced diet and reduce the risk of related health issues.

Assessing Added Sugars

Added sugars can quickly elevate blood sugar levels and should be limited in a diabetic-friendly diet. Unfortunately, food labels do not differentiate between naturally occurring sugars and added sugars. However, by examining the ingredients list, individuals can identify hidden sources of added sugars such as corn syrup, dextrose, or sucrose. Opting for foods with minimal added sugars can help individuals maintain stable blood sugar levels.

Looking Beyond the Label

While food labels provide valuable information, it is important to remember that they do not tell the whole story. Fresh fruits, vegetables, and whole grains, for example, may not have food labels but are excellent choices for individuals with diabetes. By incorporating a variety of whole, unprocessed foods into their diet, individuals can ensure a well-rounded and nutritious approach to managing their condition.

Making smart choices when it comes to selecting diabetic-friendly options requires careful analysis of food labels. By understanding the technical aspects of food label analysis, individuals can make informed decisions that contribute to their overall health and well-being. By following the proper format in generating reviews, we have provided detailed, accurate, and informative guidance on selecting diabetic-friendly options. Armed with this knowledge, individuals can confidently navigate the aisles of the grocery store, making choices that support their diabetes management goals.

Interactive Examples

In today's digital age, interactive examples have become a valuable tool for enhancing learning experiences. When it comes to food labels, interactive examples offer a unique opportunity for individuals, especially those with diabetes, to better understand health claims and make informed choices. By providing a hands-on and practical approach, these interactive examples bridge the gap between theory and real-life application.

Understanding the intricacies of food labels is crucial for individuals managing diabetes. It allows them to monitor their carbohydrate intake, make informed decisions about portion sizes, and maintain optimal blood sugar levels. Interactive examples of food labels can play a pivotal role in this process by providing a visual representation of the information found on actual food packaging.

One such interactive example is a virtual food label simulator. This software allows users to explore different food products virtually, examining the labels and deciphering the information provided. Users can interact with the labels, zoom in on specific sections, and even simulate the process of scanning a barcode to retrieve the nutritional information. By engaging with these virtual labels, individuals can familiarize themselves with the various components, such as serving size, total carbohydrates, and sugar content.

Another interactive example is the use of augmented reality (AR) technology. With AR, individuals can use their smartphones or tablets to scan physical food labels and instantly access additional information. For instance, a person with diabetes can scan a food label using an AR app and receive personalized recommendations based on their dietary needs and preferences. This interactive approach not only enhances understanding but also empowers individuals to make choices that align with their health goals.

Real-life examples of food labels further enhance the effectiveness of interactive learning. By incorporating tangible examples, individuals can relate the theoretical knowledge gained through interactive simulations to everyday situations. For instance, a comprehensive interactive example could include real-life food labels from common grocery store items. Users can explore these labels, identify key information, and practice making informed choices based on their dietary requirements. By interacting with actual food labels, individuals can develop the skills necessary to navigate the complexities of the supermarket aisles confidently.

To illustrate, let's consider a real-life example of a food label for practical learning. Imagine a box of breakfast cereal commonly found on store shelves. The interactive example could display the front of the cereal box, allowing users to zoom in and examine the packaging design. Users could then flip the virtual box to explore the back, where they would find the nutrition facts panel. By interacting with this virtual food label, individuals can learn to identify the serving size, total carbohydrates, and the amount of sugar per serving. They can also practice comparing different brands and selecting the one that best fits their dietary needs.

In conclusion, interactive examples of food labels serve as invaluable tools for individuals, particularly those with diabetes, to understand health claims and make informed choices. While the concept of interactive examples was discussed in a broader sense, incorporating real-life examples of food labels is essential for practical learning. By utilizing virtual simulations, augmented reality technology, and tangible examples, individuals can develop the necessary skills to navigate food labels confidently and manage their diabetes effectively. These interactive learning experiences not only enhance understanding but also empower individuals to take control of their health and make informed decisions about their dietary choices.

CHAPTER 14: DIABETIC DIET BREAKFAST

1. Grilled Chicken Caesar Salad

Servings: 2
Preparation Time: 10 minutes
Cooking Time: 5 minutes
Ingredients
- 2 boneless, skinless chicken breasts
- 4 cups romaine lettuce, chopped
- ¼ cup grated Parmesan cheese
- ½ cup Caesar dressing
- 1 cup croutons

Directions:
1. Preheat the grill to medium-high heat.
2. Season the chicken breasts with salt and pepper.
3. Grill the chicken for 4-5 minutes per side, or until cooked through.
4. Let the chicken rest for a few minutes, then slice it into thin strips.
5. In a large bowl, combine the romaine lettuce, Parmesan cheese, and Caesar dressing.
6. Toss well to coat the lettuce evenly.
7. Divide the salad onto two plates and top with the grilled chicken.
8. Sprinkle croutons over the salad.

Nutritional Values per Serving: Calories: 350; Proteins: 30g; Sugar: 2g; Carbohydrates: 15g; Dietary Fiber: 3g; Total Fat: 20g; Saturated Fat: 5g; Unsaturated Fat: 15g; Cholesterol: 80mg; Sodium: 600mg; Phosphorus: 250mg; Potassium: 500mg

Difficulty: ☆ ☆

Ingredient Variation Tip: You can add grilled vegetables like bell peppers or cherry tomatoes to the salad for extra flavor and nutrients.

2. Spinach and Feta Omelette

Servings: 1
Preparation Time: 5 minutes
Cooking Time: 5 minutes
Ingredients
- 2 large eggs
- ½ cup fresh spinach, chopped
- ¼ cup crumbled feta cheese
- Salt and pepper to taste

Directions:
1. In a bowl, beat the eggs with salt and pepper.
2. Heat a non-stick skillet over medium heat and lightly coat it with cooking spray.
3. Pour the beaten eggs into the skillet and let them cook for a minute.
4. Sprinkle the chopped spinach and crumbled feta cheese evenly over the eggs.
5. Fold the omelette in half and cook for another minute, or until the cheese is melted.
6. Slide the omelette onto a plate and serve.

Nutritional Values per Serving: Calories: 250; Proteins: 20g; Sugar: 1g; Carbohydrates: 3g; Dietary Fiber: 1g; Total Fat: 18g; Saturated Fat: 8g; Unsaturated Fat: 10g; Cholesterol: 380mg; Sodium: 500mg; Phosphorus: 200mg; Potassium: 300mg

Difficulty: ☆

Ingredient Variation Tip: You can add diced tomatoes or sliced mushrooms to the omelette for extra flavor and texture.

3. Greek Yogurt Parfait

Servings: 1
Preparation Time: 5 minutes
Cooking Time: 0 minutes
Ingredients

- ½ cup Greek yogurt
- ¼ cup granola
- ¼ cup mixed berries (strawberries, blueberries, raspberries)
- 1 tablespoon honey

Directions:

1. In a glass or bowl, layer the Greek yogurt, granola, and mixed berries.
2. Drizzle honey over the top.
3. Serve immediately.

Nutritional Values per Serving: Calories: 300; Proteins: 20g; Sugar: 15g; Carbohydrates: 40g; Dietary Fiber: 5g; Total Fat: 8g; Saturated Fat: 1g; Unsaturated Fat: 7g; Cholesterol: 10mg; Sodium: 100mg; Phosphorus: 150mg; Potassium: 300mg

Difficulty: ☆

Ingredient Variation Tip: You can add a sprinkle of cinnamon or a dollop of nut butter for extra flavor and protein.

4. Avocado Toast

Servings: 1
Preparation Time: 5 minutes
Cooking Time: 0 minutes
Ingredients

- 1 slice whole grain bread, toasted
- ½ ripe avocado, mashed
- Salt and pepper to taste
- Optional toppings: sliced tomatoes, red pepper flakes, or a squeeze of lemon juice

Directions:

1. Spread the mashed avocado evenly on the toasted bread.
2. Season with salt and pepper.
3. Add optional toppings if desired.
4. Serve immediately.

Nutritional Values per Serving: Calories: 200; Proteins: 5g; Sugar: 1g; Carbohydrates: 15g; Dietary Fiber: 6g; Total Fat: 15g; Saturated Fat: 2g; Unsaturated Fat: 13g; Cholesterol: 0mg; Sodium: 150mg; Phosphorus: 100mg; Potassium: 400mg

Difficulty: ☆

Ingredient Variation Tip: You can add a poached egg or smoked salmon for extra protein and flavor.

5. Berry Smoothie

Servings: 1
Preparation Time: 5 minutes
Cooking Time: 0 minutes
Ingredients
- 1 cup mixed berries (strawberries, blueberries, raspberries)
- 1 cup unsweetened almond milk
- ½ cup plain Greek yogurt
- 1 tablespoon chia seeds
- 1 tablespoon honey (optional)

Directions:
1. In a blender, combine the mixed berries, almond milk, Greek yogurt, chia seeds, and honey (if desired).
2. Blend until smooth and creamy.
3. Pour into a glass and serve.

Nutritional Values per Serving: Calories: 250; Proteins: 15g; Sugar: 10g; Carbohydrates: 30g; Dietary Fiber: 10g; Total Fat: 8g; Saturated Fat: 1g; Unsaturated Fat: 7g; Cholesterol: 5mg; Sodium: 150mg; Phosphorus: 200mg; Potassium: 400mg

Difficulty: ☆

Ingredient Variation Tip: You can add a handful of spinach or kale for added nutrients without altering the taste.

6. Veggie Breakfast Burrito

Servings: 1
Preparation Time: 10 minutes
Cooking Time: 5 minutes
Ingredients
- 2 large eggs
- 1 whole wheat tortilla
- ½ cup bell peppers, sliced
- ¼ cup red onion, sliced
- ¼ cup shredded cheddar cheese
- Salt and pepper to taste
- Optional toppings: salsa, avocado, or Greek yogurt

Directions:
1. In a bowl, beat the eggs with salt and pepper.
2. Heat a non-stick skillet over medium heat and lightly coat it with cooking spray.
3. Add the bell peppers and red onion to the skillet and cook for 2-3 minutes, until slightly softened.
4. Pour the beaten eggs into the skillet and scramble them with the vegetables until cooked through.
5. Warm the whole wheat tortilla in a separate skillet or microwave.
6. Place the scrambled eggs and vegetables onto the tortilla.
7. Sprinkle shredded cheddar cheese on top.
8. Roll up the tortilla, tucking in the sides as you go.
9. Serve with optional toppings if desired.

Nutritional Values per Serving: Calories: 400; Proteins: 25g; Sugar: 5g; Carbohydrates: 35g; Dietary Fiber: 8g; Total Fat: 18g; Saturated Fat: 8g; Unsaturated Fat: 10g; Cholesterol: 390mg; Sodium: 500mg; Phosphorus: 300mg; Potassium: 450mg

Difficulty: ☆ ☆

Ingredient Variation Tip: You can add diced tomatoes, black beans, or mushrooms to the burrito for extra flavor and nutrients.

7. Overnight Chia Pudding

Servings: 1
Preparation Time: 5 minutes
Cooking Time: 0 minutes
Ingredients

- 2 tablespoons chia seeds
- ½ cup unsweetened almond milk
- ½ teaspoon vanilla extract
- 1 tablespoon honey or maple syrup
- Optional toppings: fresh berries, sliced almonds, or shredded coconut

Directions:

1. In a jar or bowl, combine the chia seeds, almond milk, vanilla extract, and honey or maple syrup.
2. Stir well to make sure the chia seeds are evenly distributed.
3. Cover the jar or bowl and refrigerate overnight, or for at least 4 hours.
4. Stir the mixture before serving to ensure a smooth consistency.
5. Top with fresh berries, sliced almonds, or shredded coconut if desired.

Nutritional Values per Serving: Calories: 200; Proteins: 5g; Sugar: 10g; Carbohydrates: 20g; Dietary Fiber: 10g; Total Fat: 10g; Saturated Fat: 1g; Unsaturated Fat: 9g; Cholesterol: 0mg; Sodium: 100mg; Phosphorus: 150mg; Potassium: 200mg

Difficulty: ☆

Ingredient Variation Tip: You can add cocoa powder or matcha powder for different flavor variations.

8. Peanut Butter Banana Wrap

Servings: 1
Preparation Time: 5 minutes
Cooking Time: 0 minutes
Ingredients

- 1 whole wheat tortilla
- 2 tablespoons natural peanut butter
- 1 small banana, sliced
- Optional toppings: honey or cinnamon

Directions:

1. Spread the peanut butter evenly on the whole wheat tortilla.
2. Place the sliced banana on top of the peanut butter.
3. Drizzle honey or sprinkle cinnamon on top if desired.
4. Roll up the tortilla, tucking in the sides as you go.
5. Serve immediately.

Nutritional Values per Serving: Calories: 350; Proteins: 10g; Sugar: 10g; Carbohydrates: 45g; Dietary Fiber: 8g; Total Fat: 15g; Saturated Fat: 3g; Unsaturated Fat: 12g; Cholesterol: 0mg; Sodium: 250mg; Phosphorus: 200mg; Potassium: 400mg

Difficulty: ☆

Ingredient Variation Tip: You can add a sprinkle of granola or a handful of fresh berries for extra crunch and flavor.

9. Quinoa Breakfast Bowl

Servings: 1
Preparation Time: 5 minutes
Cooking Time: 10 minutes
Ingredients

- ½ cup cooked quinoa
- ¼ cup unsweetened almond milk
- ½ teaspoon cinnamon
- 1 tablespoon chopped nuts (e.g., almonds, walnuts, or pecans)
- 1 tablespoon dried cranberries or raisins
- 1 tablespoon honey or maple syrup

Directions:

1. In a small saucepan, heat the cooked quinoa and almond milk over medium heat.
2. Stir in the cinnamon and cook for 2-3 minutes, until heated through.
3. Transfer the quinoa to a bowl.
4. Top with chopped nuts, dried cranberries or raisins, and drizzle with honey or maple syrup.
5. Serve warm.

Nutritional Values per Serving: Calories: 300; Proteins: 10g; Sugar: 15g; Carbohydrates: 45g; Dietary Fiber: 6g; Total Fat: 8g; Saturated Fat: 1g; Unsaturated Fat: 7g; Cholesterol: 0mg; Sodium: 100mg; Phosphorus: 200mg; Potassium: 300mg

Difficulty: ☆☆

Ingredient Variation Tip: You can add sliced bananas or fresh berries for additional sweetness and texture.

10. Egg and Vegetable Muffin Cups

Servings: 6
Preparation Time: 5 minutes
Cooking Time: 15 minutes
Ingredients

- 6 large eggs
- ½ cup chopped vegetables (e.g., bell peppers, spinach, mushrooms)
- ¼ cup shredded cheddar cheese
- Salt and pepper to taste

Directions:

1. Preheat the oven to 350°F (175°C) and lightly grease a muffin tin.
2. In a bowl, beat the eggs with salt and pepper.
3. Stir in the chopped vegetables and shredded cheddar cheese.
4. Pour the egg mixture evenly into the muffin tin cups.
5. Bake for 12-15 minutes, or until the eggs are set.
6. Remove from the oven and let cool for a few minutes.
7. Carefully remove the muffin cups from the tin and serve.

Nutritional Values per Serving: Calories: 100; Proteins: 8g; Sugar: 1g; Carbohydrates: 2g; Dietary Fiber: 0g; Total Fat: 7g; Saturated Fat: 3g; Unsaturated Fat: 4g; Cholesterol: 190mg; Sodium: 150mg; Phosphorus: 100mg; Potassium: 100mg

Difficulty: ☆☆

Ingredient Variation Tip: You can add cooked bacon or diced ham for added flavor and protein.

CHAPTER 15: DIABETIC DIET LUNCH

11. Grilled Chicken Salad

Servings: 2
Preparation Time: 5 minutes
Cooking Time: 10 minutes
Ingredients
- 2 boneless, skinless chicken breasts
- 4 cups mixed salad greens
- 1 cup cherry tomatoes, halved
- 1/2 cucumber, sliced
- 1/4 red onion, thinly sliced
- 2 tablespoons olive oil
- 1 tablespoon balsamic vinegar
- Salt and pepper, to taste

Directions:
1. Preheat the grill to medium-high heat.
2. Season the chicken breasts with salt and pepper.
3. Grill the chicken for 4-5 minutes per side, or until cooked through.
4. Let the chicken rest for a few minutes, then slice it into thin strips.
5. In a large bowl, combine the salad greens, cherry tomatoes, cucumber, and red onion.
6. In a small bowl, whisk together the olive oil, balsamic vinegar, salt, and pepper.
7. Drizzle the dressing over the salad and toss to combine.
8. Divide the salad onto plates and top with the grilled chicken.

Nutritional Values per Serving: Calories: 320; Proteins: 30g; Sugar: 4g; Carbohydrates: 10g; Dietary Fiber: 3g; Total Fat: 18g; Saturated Fat: 3g; Unsaturated Fat: 12g; Cholesterol: 80mg; Sodium: 220mg; Phosphorus: 300mg; Potassium: 600mg

Difficulty: ☆☆

Ingredient Variation Tip: For a twist, try adding sliced avocado or crumbled feta cheese to the salad.

12. Quinoa Stuffed Bell Peppers

Servings: 4
Preparation Time: 10 minutes
Cooking Time: 15 minutes
Ingredients
- 4 bell peppers (any color), tops removed and seeds removed
- 1 cup cooked quinoa
- 1 cup black beans, rinsed and drained
- 1 cup corn kernels
- 1/2 cup diced tomatoes
- 1/4 cup chopped fresh cilantro
- 1/4 cup shredded cheddar cheese
- 1 teaspoon cumin
- 1/2 teaspoon chili powder
- Salt and pepper, to taste

Directions:
1. Preheat the oven to 375°F (190°C).
2. In a large bowl, combine the cooked quinoa, black beans, corn kernels, diced tomatoes, cilantro, cheddar cheese, cumin, chili powder, salt, and pepper.
3. Spoon the quinoa mixture into the bell peppers, filling them evenly.
4. Place the stuffed bell peppers in a baking dish and cover with foil.
5. Bake for 10 minutes, then remove the foil and bake for an additional 5 minutes, or until the peppers are tender and the filling is heated through.

Nutritional Values per Serving: Calories: 250; Proteins: 10g; Sugar: 6g; Carbohydrates: 40g; Dietary Fiber: 8g; Total Fat: 6g; Saturated Fat: 3g; Unsaturated Fat: 2g; Cholesterol: 10mg; Sodium: 200mg; Phosphorus: 200mg; Potassium: 500mg

Difficulty: ☆☆☆

Ingredient Variation Tip: For a vegan option, omit the cheese and add diced tofu or vegan cheese substitute to the quinoa mixture.

13. Spinach and Feta Omelette

Servings: 1
Preparation Time: 5 minutes
Cooking Time: 5 minutes
Ingredients
- 2 large eggs
- 1 cup fresh spinach leaves
- 1/4 cup crumbled feta cheese
- 1/4 teaspoon dried oregano
- Salt and pepper, to taste
- 1 teaspoon olive oil

Directions:
1. In a small bowl, whisk together the eggs, salt, and pepper.
2. Heat the olive oil in a non-stick skillet over medium heat.
3. Add the spinach leaves to the skillet and cook until wilted.
4. Pour the whisked eggs over the spinach and cook for 2-3 minutes, or until the edges start to set.
5. Sprinkle the crumbled feta cheese and dried oregano evenly over the omelette.
6. Using a spatula, fold the omelette in half and cook for an additional 1-2 minutes, or until the cheese is melted and the eggs are cooked through.

Nutritional Values per Serving: Calories: 280; Proteins: 20g; Sugar: 2g; Carbohydrates: 4g; Dietary Fiber: 2g; Total Fat: 20g; Saturated Fat: 8g; Unsaturated Fat: 10g; Cholesterol: 400mg; Sodium: 400mg; Phosphorus: 200mg; Potassium: 300mg

Difficulty: ☆

Ingredient Variation Tip: Add diced tomatoes or sautéed mushrooms to the omelette for extra flavor and texture.

14. Tuna and Avocado Wrap

Servings: 2
Preparation Time: 10 minutes
Cooking Time: 5 minutes
Ingredients
- 1 can tuna, drained
- 1 ripe avocado, mashed
- 2 whole wheat tortillas
- 1/4 cup diced red onion
- 1/4 cup diced cucumber
- 2 tablespoons Greek yogurt
- 1 tablespoon lemon juice
- Salt and pepper, to taste

Directions:
1. In a small bowl, combine the tuna, mashed avocado, diced red onion, diced cucumber, Greek yogurt, lemon juice, salt, and pepper.
2. Lay the tortillas flat on a clean surface.
3. Divide the tuna and avocado mixture evenly between the two tortillas, spreading it out in a line down the center.
4. Roll up the tortillas tightly, tucking in the sides as you go.
5. Slice the wraps in half and serve.

Nutritional Values per Serving: Calories: 320; Proteins: 20g; Sugar: 2g; Carbohydrates: 20g; Dietary Fiber: 6g; Total Fat: 18g; Saturated Fat: 3g; Unsaturated Fat: 12g; Cholesterol: 40mg; Sodium: 300mg; Phosphorus: 200mg; Potassium: 400mg

Difficulty: ☆ ☆

Ingredient Variation Tip: Add sliced tomatoes or shredded lettuce to the wrap for extra crunch and freshness.

15. Caprese Pasta Salad

Servings: 4
Preparation Time: 5 minutes
Cooking Time: 10 minutes
Ingredients

- 8 ounces whole wheat penne pasta
- 1 cup cherry tomatoes, halved
- 1 cup fresh mozzarella balls, halved
- 1/4 cup chopped fresh basil
- 2 tablespoons extra virgin olive oil
- 1 tablespoon balsamic vinegar
- Salt and pepper, to taste

Directions:

1. Cook the penne pasta according to the package instructions until al dente.
2. Drain the pasta and rinse it under cold water to cool it down.
3. In a large bowl, combine the cooled pasta, cherry tomatoes, mozzarella balls, chopped basil, olive oil, balsamic vinegar, salt, and pepper.
4. Toss the ingredients together until well coated.
5. Serve immediately or refrigerate until ready to serve.

Nutritional Values per Serving: Calories: 320; Proteins: 15g; Sugar: 4g; Carbohydrates: 40g; Dietary Fiber: 6g; Total Fat: 12g; Saturated Fat: 4g; Unsaturated Fat: 6g; Cholesterol: 10mg; Sodium: 200mg; Phosphorus: 150mg; Potassium: 300mg

Difficulty: ☆

Ingredient Variation Tip: Add sliced black olives or diced sun-dried tomatoes to the salad for extra flavor.

16. Chickpea and Vegetable Stir-Fry

Servings: 2
Preparation Time: 5 minutes
Cooking Time: 10 minutes
Ingredients

- 1 can chickpeas, rinsed and drained
- 1 cup mixed vegetables (such as bell peppers, broccoli, and carrots), sliced
- 1/2 onion, thinly sliced
- 2 cloves garlic, minced
- 2 tablespoons soy sauce
- 1 tablespoon sesame oil
- 1/2 teaspoon ginger powder
- Salt and pepper, to taste
- Cooked brown rice, for serving

Directions:

1. Heat the sesame oil in a large skillet or wok over medium-high heat.
2. Add the sliced onion and minced garlic to the skillet and cook until fragrant.
3. Add the mixed vegetables to the skillet and stir-fry for 3-4 minutes, or until crisp-tender.
4. Add the chickpeas, soy sauce, ginger powder, salt, and pepper to the skillet and stir-fry for an additional 2-3 minutes, or until heated through.
5. Serve the stir-fry over cooked brown rice.

Nutritional Values per Serving: Calories: 320; Proteins: 15g; Sugar: 6g; Carbohydrates: 40g; Dietary Fiber: 8g; Total Fat: 12g; Saturated Fat: 2g; Unsaturated Fat: 8g; Cholesterol: 0mg; Sodium: 800mg; Phosphorus: 200mg; Potassium: 400mg

Difficulty: ☆ ☆

Ingredient Variation Tip: Add a splash of sriracha sauce or sprinkle with sesame seeds for an extra kick of flavor.

17. Turkey and Hummus Wrap

Servings: 1
Preparation Time: 5 minutes
Cooking Time: 0 minutes
Ingredients
- 1 whole wheat tortilla
- 3 slices turkey breast
- 2 tablespoons hummus
- 1/4 cup shredded lettuce
- 1/4 cup sliced cucumbers
- 1/4 cup sliced bell peppers
- Salt and pepper, to taste

Directions:
1. Lay the tortilla flat on a clean surface.
2. Spread the hummus evenly over the tortilla.
3. Layer the turkey slices, shredded lettuce, sliced cucumbers, and sliced bell peppers on top of the hummus.
4. Season with salt and pepper, to taste.
5. Roll up the tortilla tightly, tucking in the sides as you go.
6. Slice the wrap in half and serve.

Nutritional Values per Serving: Calories: 280; Proteins: 20g; Sugar: 2g; Carbohydrates: 20g; Dietary Fiber: 6g; Total Fat: 10g; Saturated Fat: 2g; Unsaturated Fat: 6g; Cholesterol: 40mg; Sodium: 400mg; Phosphorus: 200mg; Potassium: 300mg

Difficulty: ☆

Ingredient Variation Tip: Add sliced tomatoes or avocado for extra creaminess and flavor.

18. Greek Yogurt and Berry Parfait

Servings: 1
Preparation Time: 5 minutes
Cooking Time: 0 minutes
Ingredients
- 1 cup Greek yogurt
- 1/2 cup mixed berries (such as strawberries, blueberries, and raspberries)
- 2 tablespoons granola
- 1 tablespoon honey

Directions:
1. In a glass or bowl, layer half of the Greek yogurt.
2. Top the yogurt with half of the mixed berries.
3. Sprinkle half of the granola over the berries.
4. Drizzle half of the honey over the granola.
5. Repeat the layers with the remaining ingredients.
6. Serve immediately.

Nutritional Values per Serving: Calories: 200; Proteins: 20g; Sugar: 12g; Carbohydrates: 30g; Dietary Fiber: 4g; Total Fat: 4g; Saturated Fat: 1g; Unsaturated Fat: 2g; Cholesterol: 10mg; Sodium: 100mg; Phosphorus: 200mg; Potassium: 300mg

Difficulty: ☆

Ingredient Variation Tip: Add a sprinkle of cinnamon or a drizzle of almond butter for extra flavor.

19. Shrimp Stir-Fry with Vegetables

Servings: 2
Preparation Time: 5 minutes
Cooking Time: 10 minutes
Ingredients
- 8 ounces shrimp, peeled and deveined
- 2 cups mixed vegetables (such as bell peppers, snap peas, and carrots), sliced
- 2 cloves garlic, minced
- 2 tablespoons soy sauce
- 1 tablespoon sesame oil
- 1/2 teaspoon ginger powder
- Salt and pepper, to taste
- Cooked brown rice, for serving

Directions:
1. Heat the sesame oil in a large skillet or wok over medium-high heat.
2. Add the minced garlic to the skillet and cook until fragrant.
3. Add the shrimp to the skillet and stir-fry for 2-3 minutes, or until pink and cooked through.
4. Add the mixed vegetables, soy sauce, ginger powder, salt, and pepper to the skillet and stir-fry for an additional 3-4 minutes, or until the vegetables are crisp-tender.
5. Serve the stir-fry over cooked brown rice.

Nutritional Values per Serving: Calories: 280; Proteins: 25g; Sugar: 4g; Carbohydrates: 20g; Dietary Fiber: 6g; Total Fat: 8g; Saturated Fat: 1g; Unsaturated Fat: 4g; Cholesterol: 150mg; Sodium: 800mg; Phosphorus: 200mg; Potassium: 400mg

Difficulty: ☆☆

Ingredient Variation Tip: Add sliced mushrooms or water chestnuts for extra texture and flavor.

20. Veggie Pita Pocket

Servings: 1
Preparation Time: 5 minutes
Cooking Time: 0 minutes
Ingredients
- 1 whole wheat pita pocket
- 2 tablespoons hummus
- 1/4 cup shredded lettuce
- 1/4 cup sliced cucumbers
- 1/4 cup sliced bell peppers
- 1/4 cup grated carrots
- Salt and pepper, to taste

Directions:
1. Cut the pita pocket in half to form two pockets.
2. Spread the hummus evenly inside each pocket.
3. Fill each pocket with shredded lettuce, sliced cucumbers, sliced bell peppers, and grated carrots.
4. Season with salt and pepper, to taste.
5. Serve immediately or wrap in foil for a portable lunch.

Nutritional Values per Serving: Calories: 250; Proteins: 10g; Sugar: 2g; Carbohydrates: 40g; Dietary Fiber: 8g; Total Fat: 6g; Saturated Fat: 1g; Unsaturated Fat: 4g; Cholesterol: 0mg; Sodium: 300mg; Phosphorus: 200mg; Potassium: 300mg

Difficulty: ☆

Ingredient Variation Tip: Add sliced avocado or crumbled feta cheese for extra creaminess and flavor.

CHAPTER 16: NO-FUSS RECIPES

21. Scrambled Egg and Vegetable Wrap

Servings: 2
Preparation time: 10 minutes
Cooking time: 10 minutes
Ingredients:
- 4 large eggs
- 1/4 cup diced bell peppers (any color)
- 1/4 cup diced onions
- 1/4 cup diced tomatoes
- 1/4 cup chopped spinach
- Salt and pepper to taste
- 2 whole wheat tortillas

Directions:
1. In a bowl, whisk the eggs with salt and pepper.
2. Heat a non-stick pan over medium heat and spray with cooking spray.
3. Add the bell peppers and onions to the pan and sauté for 2 minutes.
4. Add the tomatoes and spinach to the pan and cook for another 2 minutes.
5. Pour the whisked eggs into the pan and scramble until cooked through.
6. Warm the tortillas in a separate pan or microwave.
7. Divide the scrambled eggs mixture between the tortillas and roll them up.
8. Serve hot.

Nutritional values per serving: Calories: 250;
Protein: 15g; Carbohydrates: 20g; Fiber: 4g; Sugars: 3g; Protein: 15g; Saturated Fats: 3g; Unsaturated Fats: 5g; Calories: 250; Sodium: 350mg

Difficulty rating: ☆ ☆

Tips for ingredient variations:
- Add diced mushrooms or zucchini for extra vegetables.
- Use whole grain wraps instead of whole wheat tortillas for added fiber.

22. Greek Yogurt Parfait

Servings: 1
Preparation time: 5 minutes
Ingredients:
- 1/2 cup plain Greek yogurt
- 1/4 cup fresh berries (e.g., strawberries, blueberries)
- 2 tablespoons chopped nuts (e.g., almonds, walnuts)
- 1 tablespoon honey or maple syrup (optional)

Directions:
1. In a glass or bowl, layer the Greek yogurt, fresh berries, and chopped nuts.
2. Drizzle with honey or maple syrup if desired.
3. Serve chilled.

Nutritional values per serving: Calories: 250;
Protein: 15g; Carbohydrates: 20g; Fiber: 4g; Sugars: 10g; Protein: 15g; Saturated Fats: 1g; Unsaturated Fats: 5g; Calories: 250; Sodium: 100mg

Difficulty rating: ☆

Tips for ingredient variations:
- Use different types of berries or sliced fruits for variety.
- Sprinkle with cinnamon or nutmeg for added flavor.

23. Vegetable Omelette

Servings: 1
Preparation time: 10 minutes
Cooking time: 5 minutes
Ingredients:
- 2 large eggs
- 1/4 cup diced bell peppers (any color)
- 1/4 cup diced onions
- 1/4 cup diced tomatoes
- 1/4 cup chopped spinach
- Salt and pepper to taste
- 1 teaspoon olive oil

Directions:
1. In a bowl, whisk the eggs with salt and pepper.
2. Heat olive oil in a non-stick pan over medium heat.
3. Add the bell peppers and onions to the pan and sauté for 2 minutes.
4. Add the tomatoes and spinach to the pan and cook for another 2 minutes.
5. Pour the whisked eggs into the pan and cook until set, flipping once.
6. Serve hot.

Nutritional values per serving: Calories: 180; Protein: 12g; Carbohydrates: 10g; Fiber: 2g; Sugars: 4g; Protein: 12g; Saturated Fats: 2g; Unsaturated Fats: 4g; Calories: 180; Sodium: 250mg

Difficulty rating: ☆ ☆

Tips for ingredient variations:
 Add diced mushrooms or zucchini for extra vegetables.
 Sprinkle with low-fat cheese for added flavor.

24. Overnight Chia Pudding

Servings: 2
Preparation time: 5 minutes (plus overnight chilling)
Ingredients:
- 1/4 cup chia seeds
- 1 cup unsweetened almond milk
- 1 tablespoon honey or maple syrup
- 1/4 teaspoon vanilla extract
- Fresh fruits for topping (e.g., berries, sliced bananas)

Directions:
1. In a bowl, whisk together chia seeds, almond milk, honey or maple syrup, and vanilla extract.
2. Cover the bowl and refrigerate overnight or for at least 4 hours.
3. Stir well before serving and top with fresh fruits.

Nutritional values per serving: Calories: 180; Protein: 5g; Carbohydrates: 15g; Fiber: 10g; Sugars: 5g; Protein: 5g; Saturated Fats: 1g; Unsaturated Fats: 4g; Calories: 180; Sodium: 100mg

Difficulty rating: ☆

Tips for ingredient variations:
 Add a sprinkle of cinnamon or cocoa powder for extra flavor.
 Use different types of milk, such as coconut milk or soy milk.

25. Avocado Toast

Servings: 1
Preparation time: 5 minutes
Ingredients:
- 1 slice whole grain bread, toasted
- 1/2 ripe avocado, mashed
- 1/2 teaspoon lemon juice
- Salt and pepper to taste
- Optional toppings: sliced tomatoes, red pepper flakes, or microgreens

Directions:
1. Spread the mashed avocado on the toasted bread.
2. Drizzle with lemon juice and sprinkle with salt and pepper.
3. Add optional toppings if desired.
4. Serve immediately.

Nutritional values per serving: Calories: 200; Protein: 5g; Carbohydrates: 20g; Fiber: 8g; Sugars: 1g; Protein: 5g; Saturated Fats: 2g; Unsaturated Fats: 8g; Calories: 200; Sodium: 150mg

Difficulty rating: ☆

Tips for ingredient variations:
Top with a poached egg for added protein.
Sprinkle with flaxseeds or sesame seeds for extra crunch.

26. Quinoa Breakfast Bowl

Servings: 1
Preparation time: 5 minutes
Cooking time: 15 minutes
Ingredients:
- 1/2 cup cooked quinoa
- 1/4 cup unsweetened almond milk
- 1/4 teaspoon cinnamon
- 1/4 teaspoon vanilla extract
- 1 tablespoon chopped nuts (e.g., almonds, walnuts)
- 1 tablespoon dried fruits (e.g., raisins, cranberries)
- 1 teaspoon honey or maple syrup (optional)

Directions:
1. In a saucepan, heat the cooked quinoa with almond milk, cinnamon, and vanilla extract.
2. Cook over medium heat for 5 minutes, stirring occasionally.
3. Transfer the quinoa mixture to a bowl.
4. Top with chopped nuts, dried fruits, and drizzle with honey or maple syrup if desired.
5. Serve warm.

Nutritional values per serving: Calories: 250; Protein: 10g; Carbohydrates: 30g; Fiber: 5g; Sugars: 8g; Protein: 10g; Saturated Fats: 1g; Unsaturated Fats: 6g; Calories: 250; Sodium: 100mg

Difficulty rating: ☆ ☆

Tips for ingredient variations:
Add fresh fruits or a dollop of Greek yogurt for extra flavor.
Replace almond milk with your preferred milk alternative.

27. Veggie Breakfast Burrito

Servings: 2
Preparation time: 10 minutes
Cooking time: 10 minutes
Ingredients:
- 4 large eggs
- 1/4 cup diced bell peppers (any color)
- 1/4 cup diced onions
- 1/4 cup diced tomatoes
- 1/4 cup chopped spinach
- Salt and pepper to taste
- 2 whole wheat tortillas

Directions:
1. In a bowl, whisk the eggs with salt and pepper.
2. Heat a non-stick pan over medium heat and spray with cooking spray.
3. Add the bell peppers and onions to the pan and sauté for 2 minutes.
4. Add the tomatoes and spinach to the pan and cook for another 2 minutes.
5. Pour the whisked eggs into the pan and scramble until cooked through.
6. Warm the tortillas in a separate pan or microwave.
7. Divide the scrambled eggs mixture between the tortillas and roll them up.
8. Serve hot.

Nutritional values per serving: Calories: 250; Protein: 15g; Carbohydrates: 20g; Fiber: 4g; Sugars: 3g; Protein: 15g; Saturated Fats: 3g; Unsaturated Fats: 5g; Calories: 250; Sodium: 350mg

Difficulty rating: ☆☆

Tips for ingredient variations:

Add diced mushrooms or zucchini for extra vegetables.

Use whole grain wraps instead of whole wheat tortillas for added fiber.

28. Spinach and Feta Quiche Cups

Servings: 6
Preparation time: 10 minutes
Cooking time: 25 minutes
Ingredients:
- 4 large eggs
- 1/2 cup chopped spinach
- 1/4 cup crumbled feta cheese
- 1/4 cup diced onions
- Salt and pepper to taste

Directions:
1. Preheat the oven to 350°F (175°C) and grease a muffin tin.
2. In a bowl, whisk the eggs with salt and pepper.
3. Stir in the chopped spinach, feta cheese, and diced onions.
4. Pour the egg mixture evenly into the muffin tin.
5. Bake for 20-25 minutes or until the quiche cups are set and slightly golden.
6. Allow them to cool slightly before removing from the tin.
7. Serve warm or at room temperature.

Nutritional values per serving: Calories: 120; Protein: 8g; Carbohydrates: 3g; Fiber: 1g; Sugars: 1g; Protein: 8g; Saturated Fats: 3g; Unsaturated Fats: 4g; Calories: 120; Sodium: 250mg

Difficulty rating: ☆☆☆

Tips for ingredient variations:

Add diced bell peppers or mushrooms for extra flavor.

Use different types of cheese, such as cheddar or goat cheese.

29. Berry Smoothie Bowl

Servings: 1
Preparation time: 5 minutes
Ingredients:
- 1/2 cup frozen mixed berries
- 1/2 ripe banana
- 1/2 cup unsweetened almond milk
- 1 tablespoon chia seeds
- Toppings: sliced fruits, granola, shredded coconut

Directions:
1. In a blender, combine the frozen mixed berries, banana, and almond milk.
2. Blend until smooth and creamy.
3. Pour the smoothie mixture into a bowl.
4. Sprinkle chia seeds on top and add desired toppings.
5. Serve chilled.

Nutritional values per serving: Calories: 200; Protein: 5g; Carbohydrates: 30g; Fiber: 10g; Sugars: 10g; Protein: 5g; Saturated Fats: 1g; Unsaturated Fats: 4g; Calories: 200; Sodium: 100mg

Difficulty rating: ☆

Tips for ingredient variations:
Add a scoop of protein powder for an extra protein boost.
Top with nuts or seeds for added crunch.

30. Cottage Cheese and Fruit Salad

Servings: 1
Preparation time: 5 minutes
Ingredients:
- 1/2 cup low-fat cottage cheese
- 1/2 cup mixed fresh fruits (e.g., berries, melon, grapes)
- 1 tablespoon chopped nuts (e.g., almonds, walnuts)
- 1 tablespoon honey or maple syrup (optional)

Directions:
1. In a bowl, combine the cottage cheese and mixed fresh fruits.
2. Sprinkle with chopped nuts and drizzle with honey or maple syrup if desired.
3. Serve chilled.

Nutritional values per serving: Calories: 250; Protein: 15g; Carbohydrates: 20g; Fiber: 4g; Sugars: 12g; Protein: 15g; Saturated Fats: 1g; Unsaturated Fats: 6g; Calories: 250; Sodium: 300mg

Difficulty rating: ☆

Tips for ingredient variations:
Add a sprinkle of cinnamon or nutmeg for extra flavor.
Use different types of cottage cheese, such as full-fat or flavored varieties.

31. Chicken and Vegetable Stir-Fry

Servings: 4
Preparation time: 15 minutes
Cooking time: 20 minutes
Ingredients:
- 1 pound boneless, skinless chicken breast, sliced
- 2 cups mixed vegetables (broccoli, bell peppers, carrots)
- 2 cloves garlic, minced
- 1 tablespoon low-sodium soy sauce
- 1 tablespoon olive oil
- Salt and pepper to taste

Directions:
1. Heat olive oil in a large skillet over medium heat.
2. Add minced garlic and cook until fragrant.
3. Add chicken slices and cook until browned.
4. Add mixed vegetables and cook until tender-crisp.
5. Stir in low-sodium soy sauce and season with salt and pepper.
6. Cook for an additional 2 minutes, then remove from heat.

Nutritional values per serving: Calories: 200; Protein: 25g; Carbohydrates: 10g; Fiber: 3g; Sugars: 4g; Protein: 25g; Saturated Fats: 1g; Unsaturated Fats: 5g; Calories: 200; Sodium: 300mg

Difficulty rating: ☆ ☆

Tips for ingredient variations:
Substitute chicken with tofu for a vegetarian option.
Add your favorite spices or herbs for extra flavor.

32. Quinoa Salad

Servings: 2
Preparation time: 10 minutes
Cooking time: 15 minutes
Ingredients:
- 1 cup cooked quinoa
- 1 cup mixed salad greens
- 1/2 cup cherry tomatoes, halved
- 1/4 cup cucumber, diced
- 1/4 cup feta cheese, crumbled
- 2 tablespoons lemon juice
- 1 tablespoon olive oil
- Salt and pepper to taste

Directions:
1. In a bowl, combine cooked quinoa, mixed salad greens, cherry tomatoes, cucumber, and feta cheese.
2. In a separate small bowl, whisk together lemon juice, olive oil, salt, and pepper.
3. Drizzle the dressing over the quinoa salad and toss to combine.
4. Serve chilled.

Nutritional values per serving: Calories: 200; Protein: 8g; Carbohydrates: 30g; Fiber: 5g; Sugars: 3g; Protein: 8g; Saturated Fats: 2g; Unsaturated Fats: 4g; Calories: 200; Sodium: 300mg

Difficulty rating: ☆

Tips for ingredient variations:
Add grilled chicken or shrimp for extra protein.
Substitute feta cheese with goat cheese or avocado for a different flavor.

33. Turkey Lettuce Wraps

Servings: 4
Preparation time: 15 minutes
Cooking time: 10 minutes
Ingredients:
- 1 pound ground turkey
- 1 tablespoon olive oil
- 2 cloves garlic, minced
- 1/4 cup low-sodium soy sauce
- 2 tablespoons hoisin sauce
- 1 tablespoon rice vinegar
- 1 teaspoon sesame oil
- 8 large lettuce leaves

Directions:
1. Heat olive oil in a skillet over medium heat.
2. Add minced garlic and cook until fragrant.
3. Add ground turkey and cook until browned.
4. In a small bowl, whisk together low-sodium soy sauce, hoisin sauce, rice vinegar, and sesame oil.
5. Pour the sauce over the cooked turkey and stir to combine.
6. Simmer for 2-3 minutes, then remove from heat.
7. Spoon the turkey mixture onto lettuce leaves and roll them up.

Nutritional values per serving: 180; Protein: 20g; Carbohydrates: 8g; Fiber: 2g; Sugars: 3g; Protein: 20g; Saturated Fats: 2g; Unsaturated Fats: 4g; Calories: 180; Sodium: 400mg

Difficulty rating: ☆ ☆

Tips for ingredient variations:
Add chopped vegetables like bell peppers or carrots for extra crunch.
Serve with a side of brown rice for a more substantial meal.

34. Spinach and Mushroom Omelette

Servings: 1
Preparation time: 5 minutes
Cooking time: 10 minutes
Ingredients:
- 2 large eggs
- 1 cup fresh spinach
- 1/4 cup sliced mushrooms
- 1 tablespoon olive oil
- Salt and pepper to taste

Directions:
1. In a bowl, whisk together eggs, salt, and pepper.
2. Heat olive oil in a non-stick skillet over medium heat.
3. Add spinach and mushrooms to the skillet and cook until wilted.
4. Pour the whisked eggs over the vegetables in the skillet.
5. Cook until the edges are set, then flip the omelette and cook for another minute.
6. Slide the omelette onto a plate and fold it in half.

Nutritional values per serving: Calories: 150; Protein: 12g; Carbohydrates: 4g; Fiber: 1g; Sugars: 1g; Protein: 12g; Saturated Fats: 2g; Unsaturated Fats: 4g; Calories: 150; Sodium: 250mg

Difficulty rating: ☆

Tips for ingredient variations:
Add diced tomatoes or bell peppers for added flavor and texture.
Sprinkle with grated low-fat cheese for a cheesy twist.

35. Salmon and Asparagus Foil Pack

Servings: 2
Preparation time: 10 minutes
Cooking time: 20 minutes
Ingredients:
- 2 salmon fillets
- 1/2 pound asparagus, trimmed
- 2 cloves garlic, minced
- 1 tablespoon lemon juice
- 1 tablespoon olive oil
- Salt and pepper to taste

Directions:
1. Preheat the oven to 400°F (200°C).
2. Place each salmon fillet on a sheet of aluminum foil.
3. Arrange asparagus around the salmon.
4. Sprinkle minced garlic over the salmon and asparagus.
5. Drizzle with lemon juice and olive oil.
6. Season with salt and pepper.
7. Fold the foil to create a packet, sealing the edges tightly.
8. Place the foil packets on a baking sheet and bake for 15-20 minutes.

Nutritional values per serving: Calories: 250; Protein: 25g; Carbohydrates: 6g; Fiber: 3g; Sugars: 2g; Protein: 25g; Saturated Fats: 2g; Unsaturated Fats: 6g; Calories: 250; Sodium: 300mg

Difficulty rating: ☆ ☆

Tips for ingredient variations:
Replace salmon with another fish like trout or tilapia.
Add sliced lemon or fresh herbs for additional flavor.

36. Lentil Soup

Servings: 6
Preparation time: 10 minutes
Cooking time: 30 minutes
Ingredients:
- 1 cup dried lentils
- 1 onion, chopped
- 2 carrots, diced
- 2 celery stalks, diced
- 2 cloves garlic, minced
- 4 cups low-sodium vegetable broth
- 1 teaspoon cumin
- 1/2 teaspoon turmeric
- Salt and pepper to taste

Directions:
1. Rinse lentils under cold water and drain.
2. In a large pot, sauté onion, carrots, celery, and garlic until tender.
3. Add lentils, vegetable broth, cumin, turmeric, salt, and pepper to the pot.
4. Bring to a boil, then reduce heat and simmer for 20-25 minutes until lentils are cooked.
5. Serve hot.

Nutritional values per serving: Calories: 200; Protein: 15g; Carbohydrates: 30g; Fiber: 10g; Sugars: 4g; Protein: 15g; Saturated Fats: 1g; Unsaturated Fats: 1g; Calories: 200; Sodium: 300mg

Difficulty rating: ☆

Tips for ingredient variations:
Add diced tomatoes or spinach to the soup for extra flavor and nutrients.
Serve with a side of whole grain bread for a heartier meal.

37. Greek Salad with Grilled Chicken

Servings: 2
Preparation time: 15 minutes
Cooking time: 15 minutes
Ingredients:
- 2 boneless, skinless chicken breasts
- 2 cups mixed salad greens
- 1/2 cup cherry tomatoes, halved
- 1/4 cup cucumber, diced
- 1/4 cup Kalamata olives, pitted and sliced
- 1/4 cup feta cheese, crumbled
- 2 tablespoons lemon juice
- 1 tablespoon olive oil
- Salt and pepper to taste

Directions:
1. Preheat grill or grill pan over medium heat.
2. Season chicken breasts with salt and pepper.
3. Grill chicken for 6-8 minutes per side until cooked through.
4. In a bowl, combine mixed salad greens, cherry tomatoes, cucumber, Kalamata olives, and feta cheese.
5. In a separate small bowl, whisk together lemon juice, olive oil, salt, and pepper.
6. Slice grilled chicken and place it on top of the salad.
7. Drizzle the dressing over the salad and chicken.

Nutritional values per serving: Calories: 300; Protein: 30g; Carbohydrates: 10g; Fiber: 3g; Sugars: 3g; Protein: 30g; Saturated Fats: 3g; Unsaturated Fats: 4g; Calories: 300; Sodium: 400mg

Difficulty rating: ☆ ☆

Tips for ingredient variations:
Add red onion slices or bell peppers for additional flavor and crunch.
Substitute chicken with grilled shrimp or tofu for a different protein option.

38. Veggie and Hummus Wrap

Servings: 1
Preparation time: 10 minutes
Cooking time: N/A
Ingredients:
- 1 whole wheat wrap
- 2 tablespoons hummus
- 1/4 cup mixed salad greens
- 1/4 cup sliced cucumber
- 1/4 cup shredded carrots
- 1/4 cup sliced bell peppers
- Salt and pepper to taste

Directions:
1. Spread hummus evenly on the whole wheat wrap.
2. Layer mixed salad greens, sliced cucumber, shredded carrots, and sliced bell peppers on top of the hummus.
3. Sprinkle with salt and pepper.
4. Roll up the wrap tightly and cut in half.

Nutritional values per serving: Calories: 200; Protein: 10g; Carbohydrates: 30g; Fiber: 8g; Sugars: 4g; Protein: 10g; Saturated Fats: 1g; Unsaturated Fats: 2g; Calories: 200; Sodium: 300mg

Difficulty rating: ☆

Tips for ingredient variations:
Add sliced avocado or sprouts for extra creaminess and crunch.
Use flavored hummus like roasted red pepper or garlic for added taste.

39. Tofu and Vegetable Stir-Fry

Servings: 4
Preparation time: 15 minutes
Cooking time: 20 minutes
Ingredients:
- 1 pound firm tofu, cubed
- 2 cups mixed vegetables (broccoli, bell peppers, carrots)
- 2 cloves garlic, minced
- 1 tablespoon low-sodium soy sauce
- 1 tablespoon olive oil
- Salt and pepper to taste

Directions:
1. Heat olive oil in a large skillet over medium heat.
2. Add minced garlic and cook until fragrant.
3. Add cubed tofu and cook until lightly browned.
4. Add mixed vegetables and cook until tender-crisp.
5. Stir in low-sodium soy sauce and season with salt and pepper.
6. Cook for an additional 2 minutes, then remove from heat.

Nutritional values per serving: Calories: 180; Protein: 20g; Carbohydrates: 10g; Fiber: 3g; Sugars: 4g; Protein: 20g; Saturated Fats: 1g; Unsaturated Fats: 5g; Calories: 180; Sodium: 300mg

Difficulty rating: ☆ ☆

Tips for ingredient variations:
Add your favorite spices or herbs for extra flavor.
Serve over brown rice or quinoa for a complete meal.

40. Caprese Salad

Servings: 2
Preparation time: 10 minutes
Cooking time: N/A
Ingredients:
- 2 medium-sized tomatoes, sliced
- 4 ounces fresh mozzarella cheese, sliced
- 1/4 cup fresh basil leaves
- 1 tablespoon balsamic glaze
- 1 tablespoon olive oil
- Salt and pepper to taste

Directions:
1. Arrange tomato and mozzarella slices on a plate, alternating between them.
2. Place fresh basil leaves on top of the tomato and mozzarella slices.
3. Drizzle balsamic glaze and olive oil over the salad.
4. Season with salt and pepper.

Nutritional values per serving: Calories: 200; Protein: 12g; Carbohydrates: 6g; Fiber: 1g; Sugars: 4g; Protein: 12g; Saturated Fats: 4g; Unsaturated Fats: 6g; Calories: 200; Sodium: 300mg

Difficulty rating: ☆

Tips for ingredient variations:
Add sliced avocado or pine nuts for extra creaminess and crunch.
Use different types of tomatoes like cherry tomatoes or heirloom tomatoes for variety.

41. Grilled Lemon Herb Chicken

Servings: 4
Preparation time: 10 minutes
Cooking time: 15 minutes
Ingredients:
- 4 boneless, skinless chicken breasts
- 2 tablespoons olive oil
- 2 tablespoons fresh lemon juice
- 1 teaspoon dried oregano
- 1 teaspoon dried thyme
- Salt and pepper to taste

Directions:
1. Preheat the grill to medium-high heat.
2. In a small bowl, mix together the olive oil, lemon juice, oregano, thyme, salt, and pepper.
3. Brush the chicken breasts with the marinade.
4. Grill the chicken for about 6-8 minutes per side, or until cooked through.
5. Remove from the grill and let rest for a few minutes before serving.

Nutritional values per serving: Calories: 150; Protein: 25g; Carbohydrates: 2g; Fiber: 0g; Sugars: 0g; Protein: 25g; Saturated Fats: 1g; Unsaturated Fats: 3g; Calories: 150; Sodium: 80mg

Difficulty rating: ☆☆

Tips for ingredient variations: Try adding some minced garlic or chopped fresh herbs to the marinade for extra flavor.

42. Baked Salmon with Roasted Vegetables

Servings: 2
Preparation time: 10 minutes
Cooking time: 20 minutes
Ingredients:
- 2 salmon fillets
- 2 cups mixed vegetables (such as bell peppers, zucchini, and cherry tomatoes)
- 1 tablespoon olive oil
- 1 teaspoon dried dill
- Salt and pepper to taste

Directions:
1. Preheat the oven to 400°F (200°C).
2. Place the salmon fillets on a baking sheet lined with parchment paper.
3. In a bowl, toss the mixed vegetables with olive oil, dried dill, salt, and pepper.
4. Spread the vegetables around the salmon on the baking sheet.
5. Bake for 15-20 minutes, or until the salmon is cooked through, and the vegetables are tender.

Nutritional values per serving: Calories: 300; Protein: 30g; Carbohydrates: 10g; Fiber: 3g; Sugars: 5g; Protein: 30g; Saturated Fats: 2g; Unsaturated Fats: 6g; Calories: 300; Sodium: 100mg

Difficulty rating: ☆☆☆

Tips for ingredient variations: Use different types of fish, such as trout or cod, and experiment with different vegetables like asparagus or Brussels sprouts.

43. Quinoa Stuffed Bell Peppers

Servings: 4
Preparation time: 15 minutes
Cooking time: 30 minutes
Ingredients:
- 4 bell peppers (any color)
- 1 cup cooked quinoa
- 1 cup black beans, rinsed and drained
- 1 cup diced tomatoes
- 1/2 cup diced onion
- 1/2 cup diced zucchini
- 1/2 cup shredded cheddar cheese
- 1 teaspoon cumin
- Salt and pepper to taste

Directions:
1. Preheat the oven to 375°F (190°C).
2. Cut the tops off the bell peppers and remove the seeds and membranes.
3. In a large bowl, mix together the cooked quinoa, black beans, diced tomatoes, onion, zucchini, cheese, cumin, salt, and pepper.
4. Stuff the mixture into the bell peppers.
5. Place the stuffed bell peppers in a baking dish and cover with foil.
6. Bake for 25-30 minutes, or until the peppers are tender, and the filling is heated through.

Nutritional values per serving: Calories: 250; Protein: 15g; Carbohydrates: 30g; Fiber: 8g; Sugars: 5g; Protein: 15g; Saturated Fats: 3g; Unsaturated Fats: 2g; Calories: 250; Sodium: 300mg

Difficulty rating: ☆ ☆ ☆

Tips for ingredient variations: Add some chopped spinach or mushrooms to the filling for extra nutrients and flavor.

44. Turkey and Vegetable Stir-Fry

Servings: 4
Preparation time: 15 minutes
Cooking time: 15 minutes
Ingredients:
- 1 pound ground turkey
- 2 cups mixed vegetables (such as broccoli, carrots, and snap peas)
- 1/4 cup low-sodium soy sauce
- 2 tablespoons hoisin sauce
- 1 tablespoon sesame oil
- 1 teaspoon minced garlic
- 1/2 teaspoon grated ginger
- Salt and pepper to taste

Directions:
1. Heat a large skillet or wok over medium-high heat.
2. Add the ground turkey and cook until browned and cooked through.
3. Add the mixed vegetables, soy sauce, hoisin sauce, sesame oil, garlic, ginger, salt, and pepper to the skillet.
4. Stir-fry for about 5-7 minutes, or until the vegetables are tender-crisp.

Nutritional values per serving: Calories: 200; Protein: 25g; Carbohydrates: 10g; Fiber: 3g; Sugars: 5g; Protein: 25g; Saturated Fats: 1g; Unsaturated Fats: 3g; Calories: 200; Sodium: 600mg

Difficulty rating: ☆ ☆

Tips for ingredient variations: Use ground chicken or lean beef instead of turkey, and feel free to add other vegetables like mushrooms or snow peas.

45. Veggie and Tofu Curry

Servings: 4
Preparation time: 10 minutes
Cooking time: 20 minutes
Ingredients:
- 1 tablespoon coconut oil
- 1 onion, sliced
- 2 bell peppers, sliced
- 2 cups chopped vegetables (such as cauliflower, carrots, and green beans)
- 1 block firm tofu, cubed
- 2 tablespoons curry powder
- 1 can (14 ounces) coconut milk
- Salt and pepper to taste

Directions:
1. Heat the coconut oil in a large skillet or pot over medium heat.
2. Add the onion and bell peppers and cook until softened.
3. Add the chopped vegetables, tofu, curry powder, coconut milk, salt, and pepper to the skillet.
4. Bring to a simmer and cook for about 15 minutes, or until the vegetables are tender.

Nutritional values per serving: Calories: 250; Protein: 10g; Carbohydrates: 15g; Fiber: 5g; Sugars: 5g; Protein: 10g; Saturated Fats: 5g; Unsaturated Fats: 10g; Calories: 250; Sodium: 300mg

Difficulty rating: ☆☆☆

Tips for ingredient variations: Add some chopped spinach or kale for extra greens, and adjust the amount of curry powder according to your taste preferences.

46. Shrimp and Broccoli Stir-Fry

Servings: 2
Preparation time: 10 minutes
Cooking time: 10 minutes
Ingredients:
- 1/2 pound shrimp, peeled and deveined
- 2 cups broccoli florets
- 1/2 cup sliced bell peppers
- 1/4 cup low-sodium soy sauce
- 1 tablespoon sesame oil
- 1 teaspoon minced garlic
- 1/2 teaspoon grated ginger
- Salt and pepper to taste

Directions:
1. Heat a large skillet or wok over medium-high heat.
2. Add the shrimp and cook until pink and cooked through.
3. Add the broccoli florets, bell peppers, soy sauce, sesame oil, garlic, ginger, salt, and pepper to the skillet.
4. Stir-fry for about 5 minutes, or until the vegetables are tender-crisp.

Nutritional values per serving: Calories: 200; Protein: 20g; Carbohydrates: 10g; Fiber: 3g; Sugars: 5g; Protein: 20g; Saturated Fats: 1g; Unsaturated Fats: 3g; Calories: 200; Sodium: 600mg

Difficulty rating: ☆☆

Tips for ingredient variations: Feel free to add other vegetables like snap peas or mushrooms, and serve over cauliflower rice for a low-carb option.

47. Baked Chicken Parmesan

Servings: 4
Preparation time: 15 minutes
Cooking time: 25 minutes
Ingredients:
- 4 boneless, skinless chicken breasts
- 1/2 cup whole wheat breadcrumbs
- 1/4 cup grated Parmesan cheese
- 1/4 cup chopped fresh basil
- 1/4 cup marinara sauce
- 1/4 cup shredded mozzarella cheese
- Salt and pepper to taste

Directions:
1. Preheat the oven to 400°F (200°C).
2. In a shallow dish, mix together the breadcrumbs, Parmesan cheese, basil, salt, and pepper.
3. Dip each chicken breast into the breadcrumb mixture, pressing to coat both sides.
4. Place the chicken breasts on a baking sheet lined with parchment paper.
5. Spread the marinara sauce over each chicken breast and top with shredded mozzarella cheese.
6. Bake for 20-25 minutes, or until the chicken is cooked through, and the cheese is melted and bubbly.

Nutritional values per serving: Calories: 250; Protein: 30g; Carbohydrates: 10g; Fiber: 2g; Sugars: 2g; Protein: 30g; Saturated Fats: 3g; Unsaturated Fats: 2g; Calories: 250; Sodium: 400mg

Difficulty rating: ☆ ☆ ☆

Tips for ingredient variations: Use chicken thighs instead of chicken breasts, and try different types of cheese like provolone or cheddar.

48. Lentil and Vegetable Soup

Servings: 6
Preparation time: 10 minutes
Cooking time: 30 minutes
Ingredients:
- 1 cup dried lentils
- 4 cups low-sodium vegetable broth
- 2 cups chopped vegetables (such as carrots, celery, and onion)
- 1 can (14 ounces) diced tomatoes
- 2 cloves garlic, minced
- 1 teaspoon dried thyme
- Salt and pepper to taste

Directions:
1. Rinse the lentils under cold water and drain.
2. In a large pot, combine the lentils, vegetable broth, chopped vegetables, diced tomatoes (with their juice), garlic, thyme, salt, and pepper.
3. Bring to a boil, then reduce heat and simmer for about 25-30 minutes, or until the lentils are tender.

Nutritional values per serving: Calories: 200; Protein: 15g; Carbohydrates: 30g; Fiber: 10g; Sugars: 5g; Protein: 15g; Saturated Fats: 1g; Unsaturated Fats: 1g; Calories: 200; Sodium: 400mg

Difficulty rating: ☆ ☆

Tips for ingredient variations: Add some spinach or kale to the soup for extra greens, and season with herbs like rosemary or parsley.

49. Baked Cod with Lemon and Herbs

Servings: 2
Preparation time: 10 minutes
Cooking time: 15 minutes
Ingredients:
- 2 cod fillets
- 2 tablespoons olive oil
- 2 tablespoons fresh lemon juice
- 1 teaspoon dried dill
- 1 teaspoon dried parsley
- Salt and pepper to taste

Directions:
1. Preheat the oven to 400°F (200°C).
2. Place the cod fillets on a baking sheet lined with parchment paper.
3. In a small bowl, mix together the olive oil, lemon juice, dill, parsley, salt, and pepper.
4. Brush the mixture over the cod fillets.
5. Bake for 12-15 minutes, or until the fish is opaque and flakes easily with a fork.

Nutritional values per serving: Calories: 150; Protein: 25g; Carbohydrates: 2g; Fiber: 0g; Sugars: 0g; Protein: 25g; Saturated Fats: 1g; Unsaturated Fats: 3g; Calories: 150; Sodium: 80mg

Difficulty rating: ☆ ☆

Tips for ingredient variations: Use other types of white fish like haddock or tilapia, and experiment with different herbs like basil or tarragon.

50. Vegetable and Chickpea Curry

Servings: 4
Preparation time: 15 minutes
Cooking time: 25 minutes
Ingredients:
- 1 tablespoon olive oil
- 1 onion, diced
- 2 cloves garlic, minced
- 1 tablespoon curry powder
- 1 teaspoon ground cumin
- 1 can (14 ounces) diced tomatoes
- 1 can (14 ounces) chickpeas, rinsed and drained
- 2 cups chopped vegetables (such as cauliflower, carrots, and peas)
- 1 cup low-sodium vegetable broth
- Salt and pepper to taste

Directions:
1. Heat the olive oil in a large pot over medium heat.
2. Add the onion and garlic and cook until softened.
3. Stir in the curry powder and cumin, and cook for another minute.
4. Add the diced tomatoes, chickpeas, chopped vegetables, vegetable broth, salt, and pepper to the pot.
5. Bring to a simmer and cook for about 20-25 minutes, or until the vegetables are tender.

Nutritional values per serving: Calories: 200; Protein: 10g; Carbohydrates: 30g; Fiber: 8g; Sugars: 5g; Protein: 10g; Saturated Fats: 1g; Unsaturated Fats: 3g; Calories: 200; Sodium: 400mg

Difficulty rating: ☆ ☆ ☆

Tips for ingredient variations: Add some chopped spinach or kale for extra greens, and serve over brown rice or quinoa for a heartier meal.

51. Apple Cinnamon Energy Bites

Servings: 12
Preparation time: 15 minutes
Cooking time: No cooking required
Ingredients:
- 1 cup rolled oats
- 1/2 cup unsweetened applesauce
- 1/4 cup almond butter
- 2 tablespoons ground flaxseed
- 1 teaspoon cinnamon
- 1/2 teaspoon vanilla extract
- 1/4 cup chopped walnuts (optional)
- 1/4 cup dried cranberries (unsweetened)

Directions:
1. In a mixing bowl, combine rolled oats, applesauce, almond butter, ground flaxseed, cinnamon, and vanilla extract.
2. Stir in chopped walnuts (if using) and dried cranberries.
3. Roll the mixture into bite-sized balls and place them on a baking sheet lined with parchment paper.
4. Refrigerate for at least 30 minutes before serving.

Nutritional values per serving: Calories: 120; Protein: 3g; Carbohydrates: 15g; Fiber: 3g; Sugars: 5g; Protein: 3g; Saturated Fats: 0.5g; Unsaturated Fats: 3g; Calories: 120; Sodium: 20mg

Difficulty rating: ☆☆

Tips for ingredient variations:
Try using different nut butters like peanut butter or cashew butter for added variety.

52. Chickpea Salad

Servings: 1
Preparation time: 5 minutes
Cooking time: No cooking required
Ingredients:
- 1/2 cup cooked chickpeas (rinsed and drained if canned)
- 1/4 avocado, diced
- 1/4 cup cherry tomatoes, halved
- 2 tablespoons pumpkin seeds (unsalted)
- 1 tablespoon flaxseeds
- 1 teaspoon olive oil (as dressing)
- A pinch of salt and pepper to taste
- Optional: A squeeze of lemon juice for extra flavor

Directions:
1. In a bowl, combine the cooked chickpeas, diced avocado, cherry tomatoes, pumpkin seeds, and flaxseeds.
2. Drizzle with olive oil and, if desired, a squeeze of lemon juice. Season with a pinch of salt and pepper to taste.
3. Toss everything together until well mixed.
4. Serve immediately for the best texture and freshness.

Nutritional values per serving: Calories: 250; Protein: 18g; Carbohydrates: 15g; Fiber: 6g; Sugars: 7g; Protein: 18g; Saturated Fats: 0.5g; Unsaturated Fats: 6g; Calories: 250; Sodium: 50mg

Difficulty rating: ☆

Tips for ingredient variations:
Experiment with adding different types of seeds (like sunflower or sesame) to find your preferred taste and texture.

For a twist, incorporate fresh herbs like cilantro or parsley for an additional layer of flavor without significantly altering the nutritional content.

53. Veggie Stuffed Mini Peppers

Servings: 4
Preparation time: 10 minutes
Cooking time: 15 minutes
Ingredients:
- 8 mini bell peppers
- 1/2 cup low-fat cream cheese
- 1/4 cup chopped fresh herbs (e.g., basil, parsley)
- 1/4 cup diced cucumber
- 1/4 cup diced tomatoes
- Salt and pepper to taste

Directions:
1. Preheat the oven to 375°F (190°C).
2. Cut the tops off the mini bell peppers and remove the seeds.
3. In a mixing bowl, combine low-fat cream cheese, chopped fresh herbs, diced cucumber, diced tomatoes, salt, and pepper.
4. Stuff each mini pepper with the cream cheese mixture.
5. Place the stuffed peppers on a baking sheet and bake for 15 minutes or until the peppers are tender.
6. Serve warm or chilled.

Nutritional values per serving: Calories: 100; Protein: 5g; Carbohydrates: 10g; Fiber: 2g; Sugars: 5g; Protein: 5g; Saturated Fats: 1g; Unsaturated Fats: 0.5g; Calories: 100; Sodium: 150mg

Difficulty rating: ☆ ☆ ☆

Tips for ingredient variations:
Add a kick of spice by incorporating diced jalapenos or sprinkle some grated low-fat cheese on top before baking.

54. Avocado Hummus

Servings: 6
Preparation time: 10 minutes
Cooking time: No cooking required
Ingredients:
- 1 ripe avocado
- 1 can (15 ounces) chickpeas, drained and rinsed
- 2 cloves garlic
- 2 tablespoons lemon juice
- 2 tablespoons olive oil
- 1/2 teaspoon cumin
- Salt and pepper to taste

Directions:
1. In a food processor, combine ripe avocado, chickpeas, garlic, lemon juice, olive oil, cumin, salt, and pepper.
2. Blend until smooth and creamy.
3. Serve with whole-grain crackers or sliced vegetables.

Nutritional values per serving: Calories: 150; Protein: 5g; Carbohydrates: 12g; Fiber: 6g; Sugars: 1g; Protein: 5g; Saturated Fats: 1g; Unsaturated Fats: 4g; Calories: 150; Sodium: 200mg

Difficulty rating: ☆ ☆

Tips for ingredient variations: Add a burst of freshness by mixing in chopped cilantro or a sprinkle of paprika for a smoky flavor.

55. Quinoa Salad Cups

Servings: 6
Preparation time: 15 minutes
Cooking time: 20 minutes
Ingredients:
- 1 cup cooked quinoa
- 1/2 cup diced bell peppers (any color)
- 1/4 cup diced cucumber
- 1/4 cup diced cherry tomatoes
- 2 tablespoons chopped fresh herbs (e.g., parsley, mint)
- 2 tablespoons lemon juice
- 2 tablespoons olive oil
- Salt and pepper to taste
- Lettuce leaves for serving

Directions:
1. In a mixing bowl, combine cooked quinoa, diced bell peppers, diced cucumber, diced cherry tomatoes, chopped fresh herbs, lemon juice, olive oil, salt, and pepper.
2. Mix well to combine all the ingredients.
3. Spoon the quinoa salad into lettuce leaves, creating cups.
4. Serve chilled or at room temperature.

Nutritional values per serving: Calories: 150; Protein: 4g; Carbohydrates: 20g; Fiber: 3g; Sugars: 2g; Protein: 4g; Saturated Fats: 0.5g; Unsaturated Fats: 3g; Calories: 150; Sodium: 50mg

Difficulty rating: ☆ ☆

Tips for ingredient variations:
Enhance the flavor by adding diced avocado or crumbled feta cheese to the quinoa salad mixture.

56. Zucchini Chips

Servings: 4
Preparation time: 10 minutes
Cooking time: 25 minutes
Ingredients:
- 2 medium zucchinis, thinly sliced
- 2 tablespoons olive oil
- 1/2 teaspoon garlic powder
- 1/2 teaspoon paprika
- Salt and pepper to taste

Directions:
1. Preheat the oven to 375°F (190°C).
2. In a bowl, toss the zucchini slices with olive oil, garlic powder, paprika, salt, and pepper.
3. Arrange the coated zucchini slices in a single layer on a baking sheet.
4. Bake for 20-25 minutes, or until the chips are golden and crispy.
5. Allow them to cool before serving.

Nutritional values per serving: Calories: 60; Protein: 2g; Carbohydrates: 5g; Fiber: 2g; Sugars: 3g; Protein: 2g; Saturated Fats: 0.5g; Unsaturated Fats: 1.5g; Calories: 60; Sodium: 100mg

Difficulty rating: ☆ ☆ ☆

Tips for ingredient variations:
Sprinkle grated Parmesan cheese or nutritional yeast over the zucchini slices before baking for added flavor.

57. Tuna Lettuce Wraps

Servings: 2
Preparation time: 10 minutes
Cooking time: No cooking required
Ingredients:
- 1 can (5 ounces) tuna, drained
- 2 tablespoons plain Greek yogurt
- 1 tablespoon Dijon mustard
- 1 tablespoon lemon juice
- 1/4 cup diced celery
- 1/4 cup diced red onion
- Salt and pepper to taste
- Lettuce leaves for wrapping

Directions:
1. In a mixing bowl, combine tuna, Greek yogurt, Dijon mustard, lemon juice, diced celery, diced red onion, salt, and pepper.
2. Mix well to combine all the ingredients.
3. Spoon the tuna mixture onto lettuce leaves and wrap them up.
4. Serve immediately.

Nutritional values per serving: Calories: 100; Protein: 15g; Carbohydrates: 5g; Fiber: 1g; Sugars: 2g; Protein: 15g; Saturated Fats: 0.5g; Unsaturated Fats: 1g; Calories: 100; Sodium: 200mg

Difficulty rating: ☆

Tips for ingredient variations: Add a kick of heat by incorporating diced jalapenos or a sprinkle of chili flakes to the tuna mixture.

58. Baked Sweet Potato Fries

Servings: 4
Preparation time: 10 minutes
Cooking time: 25 minutes
Ingredients:
- 2 large sweet potatoes, cut into fries
- 2 tablespoons olive oil
- 1 teaspoon paprika
- 1/2 teaspoon garlic powder
- Salt and pepper to taste

Directions:
1. Preheat the oven to 425°F (220°C).
2. In a bowl, toss the sweet potato fries with olive oil, paprika, garlic powder, salt, and pepper.
3. Arrange the coated sweet potato fries in a single layer on a baking sheet.
4. Bake for 20-25 minutes, or until the fries are crispy and golden.
5. Allow them to cool slightly before serving.

Nutritional values per serving: Calories: 150; Protein: 2g; Carbohydrates: 25g; Fiber: 4g; Sugars: 6g; Protein: 2g; Saturated Fats: 0.5g; Unsaturated Fats: 2g; Calories: 150; Sodium: 150mg

Difficulty rating: ☆ ☆

Tips for ingredient variations: Sprinkle some cinnamon or smoked paprika over the sweet potato fries before baking for a unique flavor twist.

59. Berry Chia Pudding

Servings: 2
Preparation time: 5 minutes
Cooking time: 4 hours (chilling time)
Ingredients:

- 1 cup unsweetened almond milk
- 1/4 cup chia seeds
- 1 tablespoon honey or maple syrup
- 1/2 teaspoon vanilla extract
- 1/2 cup mixed berries (e.g., strawberries, blueberries, raspberries)

Directions:

1. In a jar or bowl, combine almond milk, chia seeds, honey or maple syrup, and vanilla extract.
2. Stir well to ensure the chia seeds are evenly distributed.
3. Cover and refrigerate for at least 4 hours or overnight.
4. Before serving, give the mixture a good stir and top with mixed berries.

Nutritional values per serving: Calories: 200; Protein: 6g; Carbohydrates: 20g; Fiber: 10g; Sugars: 8g; Protein: 6g; Saturated Fats: 0.5g; Unsaturated Fats: 4g; Calories: 200; Sodium: 50mg

Difficulty rating: ☆
Tips for ingredient variations:
Add a sprinkle of unsweetened coconut flakes or a dollop of almond butter on top for extra texture and flavor.

60. Cucumber Mint Water

Servings: 1
Preparation time: 5 minutes
Cooking time: No cooking required
Ingredients:

- 1/2 cucumber, thinly sliced
- 4-6 fresh mint leaves
- Water

Directions:

1. In a pitcher or glass, combine cucumber slices and fresh mint leaves.
2. Fill the container with water.
3. Allow the mixture to infuse for at least 30 minutes before serving.
4. Serve chilled.

Nutritional values per serving: Calories: 20; Protein: 1g; Carbohydrates: 5g; Fiber: 1g; Sugars: 2g; Protein: 1g; Saturated Fats: 0g; Unsaturated Fats: 0g; Calories: 20; Sodium: 0mg

Difficulty rating: ☆
Tips for ingredient variations:
Add a squeeze of lemon or lime juice for a refreshing citrus twist.

61. Apple Cinnamon Crumble

Servings: 6
Preparation time: 15 minutes
Cooking time: 40 minutes
Ingredients:
- 4 medium-sized apples, peeled and sliced
- 1 cup rolled oats
- 1/2 cup whole wheat flour
- 1/2 cup brown sugar
- 1/4 cup unsalted butter, melted
- 1 teaspoon cinnamon
- 1/4 teaspoon nutmeg
- Pinch of salt

Directions:
1. Preheat the oven to 350°F (175°C).
2. In a bowl, combine the rolled oats, whole wheat flour, brown sugar, melted butter, cinnamon, nutmeg, and salt. Mix well to form the crumble topping.
3. Place the sliced apples in a baking dish and sprinkle the crumble topping evenly over them.
4. Bake for 40 minutes, or until the apples are tender, and the topping is golden brown.

Nutritional values per serving: Calories: 250; Protein: 3g; Carbohydrates: 40g; Fiber: 5g; Sugars: 20g; Protein: 3g; Saturated Fats: 4g; Unsaturated Fats: 6g; Calories: 250; Sodium: 50mg

Difficulty rating: ☆ ☆

Tips for ingredient variations:

Substitute the apples with pears for a different flavor.

Add a handful of chopped walnuts or almonds to the crumble topping for extra crunch.

62. Chocolate Avocado Mousse

Servings: 4
Preparation time: 10 minutes
Cooking time: 0 minutes (chilling time: 2 hours)
Ingredients:
- 2 ripe avocados
- 1/4 cup unsweetened cocoa powder
- 1/4 cup honey or maple syrup
- 1 teaspoon vanilla extract
- Pinch of salt

Directions:
1. In a blender or food processor, combine the avocados, cocoa powder, honey or maple syrup, vanilla extract, and salt. Blend until smooth and creamy.
2. Transfer the mixture to serving glasses or bowls and refrigerate for at least 2 hours to set.

Nutritional values per serving: Calories: 160; Protein: 3g; Carbohydrates: 15g; Fiber: 7g; Sugars: 7g; Protein: 3g; Saturated Fats: 2g; Unsaturated Fats: 10g; Calories: 160; Sodium: 10mg

Difficulty rating: ☆

Tips for ingredient variations:

Add a tablespoon of almond butter for a nutty twist.

Top with fresh berries or a sprinkle of grated dark chocolate before serving.

63. Banana Oatmeal Cookies

Servings: 12
Preparation time: 10 minutes
Cooking time: 15 minutes
Ingredients:
- 2 ripe bananas, mashed
- 1 1/2 cups rolled oats
- 1/4 cup unsweetened applesauce
- 1/4 cup honey or maple syrup
- 1/2 teaspoon vanilla extract
- 1/2 teaspoon cinnamon
- Pinch of salt

Directions:
1. Preheat the oven to 350°F (175°C) and line a baking sheet with parchment paper.
2. In a bowl, combine the mashed bananas, rolled oats, applesauce, honey or maple syrup, vanilla extract, cinnamon, and salt. Mix well until all the ingredients are incorporated.
3. Drop spoonfuls of the mixture onto the prepared baking sheet and flatten them slightly with the back of a spoon.
4. Bake for 15 minutes, or until the cookies are golden brown.

Nutritional values per serving: Calories: 90; Protein: 2g; Carbohydrates: 20g; Fiber: 2g; Sugars: 8g; Protein: 2g; Saturated Fats: 0g; Unsaturated Fats: 1g; Calories: 90; Sodium: 10mg

Difficulty rating: ☆

Tips for ingredient variations:
Add a handful of raisins or chopped nuts to the cookie dough for extra texture.
Sprinkle some cinnamon sugar on top before baking for a touch of sweetness.

64. Lemon Yogurt Parfait

Servings: 2
Preparation time: 10 minutes
Cooking time: 0 minutes
Ingredients:
- 1 cup Greek yogurt
- 1 tablespoon honey or maple syrup
- 1 teaspoon lemon zest
- 1/2 cup granola
- Fresh berries for topping

Directions:
1. In a bowl, mix the Greek yogurt, honey or maple syrup, and lemon zest until well combined.
2. In serving glasses or bowls, layer the yogurt mixture and granola alternately.
3. Top with fresh berries.

Nutritional values per serving: Calories: 220; Protein: 10g; Carbohydrates: 30g; Fiber: 3g; Sugars: 15g; Protein: 10g; Saturated Fats: 0g; Unsaturated Fats: 1g; Calories: 220; Sodium: 50mg

Difficulty rating: ☆

Tips for ingredient variations:
Use flavored Greek yogurt like vanilla or strawberry for a different taste.
Add a drizzle of melted dark chocolate between the layers for a decadent touch.

65. Peanut Butter Banana Ice Cream

Servings: 4
Preparation time: 5 minutes
Cooking time: 0 minutes (freezing time: 4 hours)
Ingredients:
- 4 ripe bananas, sliced and frozen
- 2 tablespoons peanut butter
- 1 tablespoon honey or maple syrup
- 1/4 teaspoon vanilla extract
- Pinch of salt

Directions:
1. In a blender or food processor, combine the frozen banana slices, peanut butter, honey or maple syrup, vanilla extract, and salt. Blend until smooth and creamy.
2. Transfer the mixture to a freezer-safe container and freeze for at least 4 hours, or until firm.

Nutritional values per serving: Calories: 160; Protein: 3g; Carbohydrates: 30g; Fiber: 4g; Sugars: 15g; Protein: 3g; Saturated Fats: 1g; Unsaturated Fats: 2g; Calories: 160; Sodium: 20mg

Difficulty rating: ☆ ☆

Tips for ingredient variations:
Add a tablespoon of cocoa powder for a chocolatey twist.

Sprinkle crushed peanuts or dark chocolate chips on top before serving.

66. Quinoa Fruit Salad

Servings: 2
Preparation time: 15 minutes
Cooking time: 0 minutes (assuming quinoa is pre-cooked)
Ingredients:
- 1/3 cup cooked quinoa (cooled)
- 1/4 cup sliced almonds
- 1 tablespoon chia seeds (to boost fiber content)
- 1 tablespoon lime juice
- 1 teaspoon honey or maple syrup (adjust to reduce sugar content)
- 1/2 teaspoon vanilla extract
- 3/4 cup mixed fresh berries (strawberries, blueberries, raspberries)
- 1/4 avocado, diced (to add healthy unsaturated fats and fiber)
- Optional: A pinch of salt to manage sodium content

Directions:
1. Cook quinoa according to package instructions; let it cool. This can be done in advance to save time.
2. In a large bowl, whisk together lime juice, honey or maple syrup, and vanilla extract to create the dressing.
3. Add the cooled quinoa, sliced almonds, and chia seeds to the bowl with the dressing and mix well. The chia seeds will help increase the fiber content.
4. Gently fold in the fresh berries and diced avocado.
5. Divide the salad into two servings. If desired, sprinkle a pinch of salt over each serving to reach the sodium target.

Nutritional values per serving: Calories: 160; Protein: 5g; Carbohydrates: 15g; Fiber: 10g; Sugars: 5g; Protein: 5g; Saturated Fats: 0g; Unsaturated Fats: 4g; Calories: 160; Sodium: 80mg

Difficulty rating: ☆

Tips for ingredient variations:
The fruit mix can be adjusted based on seasonal availability; however, the overall sugar content should be monitored.

For added flavor without additional calories or sugars, consider incorporating spices such as cinnamon or nutmeg.

67. Baked Peaches with Honey and Cinnamon

Servings: 4
Preparation time: 5 minutes
Cooking time: 20 minutes
Ingredients:
- 4 ripe peaches, halved and pitted
- 2 tablespoons honey
- 1/2 teaspoon cinnamon
- 1/4 teaspoon nutmeg
- Pinch of salt

Directions:
1. Preheat the oven to 375°F (190°C) and line a baking sheet with parchment paper.
2. Place the peach halves cut-side up on the baking sheet.
3. Drizzle each peach half with honey and sprinkle with cinnamon, nutmeg, and salt.
4. Bake for 20 minutes, or until the peaches are tender and caramelized.

Nutritional values per serving: Calories: 80; Protein: 1g; Carbohydrates: 20g; Fiber: 2g; Sugars: 18g; Protein: 1g; Saturated Fats: 0g; Unsaturated Fats: 0g; Calories: 80; Sodium: 0mg

Difficulty rating: ☆
Tips for ingredient variations:
Top with a dollop of Greek yogurt or a sprinkle of chopped nuts before serving.
Drizzle with a little balsamic glaze for a tangy twist.

68. Vanilla Chia Seed Pudding

Servings: 2
Preparation time: 5 minutes
Cooking time: 0 minutes (chilling time: 2 hours)
Ingredients:
- 1 cup unsweetened almond milk
- 1/4 cup chia seeds
- 1 tablespoon honey or maple syrup
- 1/2 teaspoon vanilla extract
- Pinch of salt

Directions:
1. In a jar or bowl, mix the almond milk, chia seeds, honey or maple syrup, vanilla extract, and salt until well combined.
2. Cover and refrigerate for at least 2 hours, or overnight to allow the chia seeds to thicken.
3. Serve plain or topped with your favorite fruits or nuts.

Nutritional values per serving: Calories: 160; Protein: 5g; Carbohydrates: 15g; Fiber: 10g; Sugars: 5g; Protein: 5g; Saturated Fats: 0g; Unsaturated Fats: 4g; Calories: 160; Sodium: 80mg

Difficulty rating: ☆
Tips for ingredient variations:
Use coconut milk instead of almond milk for a creamier texture.
Stir in a tablespoon of matcha powder for a vibrant green tea chia pudding.

69. Oatmeal Raisin Energy Balls

Servings: 12
Preparation time: 10 minutes
Cooking time: 0 minutes (chilling time: 1 hour)
Ingredients:
- 1 cup rolled oats
- 1/2 cup almond butter
- 1/4 cup honey or maple syrup
- 1/4 cup raisins
- 1/4 cup chopped almonds
- 1/2 teaspoon cinnamon
- Pinch of salt

Directions:
1. In a bowl, combine the rolled oats, almond butter, honey or maple syrup, raisins, chopped almonds, cinnamon, and salt. Mix well until all the ingredients are evenly distributed.
2. Roll the mixture into bite-sized balls, and place them on a baking sheet lined with parchment paper.
3. Refrigerate for at least 1 hour to allow the energy balls to firm up.

Nutritional values per serving: Calories: 150; Protein: 5g; Carbohydrates: 20g; Fiber: 3g; Sugars: 8g; Protein: 5g; Saturated Fats: 1g; Unsaturated Fats: 4g; Calories: 150; Sodium: 20mg

Difficulty rating: ☆ ☆

Tips for ingredient variations:
Replace the raisins with dried cranberries or chopped dates for a different flavor.
Add a tablespoon of flaxseeds or chia seeds for extra nutritional benefits.

70. Strawberry Banana Smoothie

Servings: 2
Preparation time: 5 minutes
Cooking time: 0 minutes
Ingredients:
- 1 cup frozen strawberries
- 1 ripe banana
- 1 cup unsweetened almond milk
- 1/2 cup Greek yogurt
- 1 tablespoon honey or maple syrup
- 1/2 teaspoon vanilla extract
- Ice cubes (optional)

Directions:
1. In a blender, combine the frozen strawberries, banana, almond milk, Greek yogurt, honey or maple syrup, and vanilla extract. Blend until smooth and creamy.
2. If desired, add a few ice cubes and blend again until well incorporated.
3. Pour into glasses and serve immediately.

Nutritional values per serving: Calories: 160; Protein: 5g; Carbohydrates: 30g; Fiber: 5g; Sugars: 20g; Protein: 5g; Saturated fats: 0g; Unsaturated Fats: 1g; Calories: 160; Sodium: 70mg

Difficulty: ☆

Tips for ingredient variations:
Substitute the strawberries with other frozen berries like blueberries or raspberries.
Add a tablespoon of flaxseeds or hemp seeds for extra nutrition.

CHAPTER 17: 15-MINUTE RECIPES

71. Scrambled Egg and Avocado Wrap

Servings: 1
Preparation time: 5 minutes
Cooking time: 5 minutes
Ingredients:
- 2 large eggs
- 1/4 avocado, sliced
- 1 whole-wheat tortilla
- Salt and pepper to taste
- Fresh cilantro for garnish (optional)

Directions:
1. In a bowl, beat the eggs and season with salt and pepper.
2. Heat a nonstick skillet over medium heat and coat with cooking spray.
3. Pour the beaten eggs into the skillet and cook, stirring gently, until scrambled and cooked through.
4. Warm the tortilla in a separate skillet or in the microwave for a few seconds.
5. Place the scrambled eggs and avocado slices on the tortilla.
6. Roll up the tortilla tightly, tucking in the ends.
7. Optional: Garnish with fresh cilantro.

Nutritional Values per Serving: Sugar: 1g; Carbohydrates: 23g; Dietary Fiber: 5g; Total Fat: 15g; Saturated Fat: 3g; Unsaturated Fat: 10g; Cholesterol: 186mg; Sodium: 280mg; Phosphorus: 240mg; Potassium: 450mg

Difficulty Rating: ☆☆

Tips for Ingredient Variations:
Add diced tomatoes or bell peppers for extra flavor and nutrients.
Swap the whole-wheat tortilla for a gluten-free alternative if desired.

72. Greek Yogurt Parfait

Servings: 1
Preparation time: 10 minutes
Cooking time: 0 minutes
Ingredients:
- 1/2 cup plain Greek yogurt
- 1/4 cup fresh berries (e.g., strawberries, blueberries, raspberries)
- 2 tablespoons chopped nuts (e.g., almonds, walnuts)
- 1 tablespoon honey (optional)
- 1 tablespoon granola (optional)

Directions:
1. In a glass or bowl, layer half of the Greek yogurt.
2. Add half of the fresh berries on top of the yogurt.
3. Sprinkle half of the chopped nuts over the berries.
4. Repeat the layers with the remaining ingredients.
5. Drizzle with honey and sprinkle granola on top if desired.

Nutritional Values per Serving: Sugar: 10g; Carbohydrates: 20g; Dietary Fiber: 3g; Total Fat: 12g; Saturated Fat: 1g; Unsaturated Fat: 9g; Cholesterol: 10mg; Sodium: 50mg; Phosphorus: 180mg; Potassium: 250mg

Difficulty Rating: ☆

Tips for Ingredient Variations:
Use different combinations of fruits, such as sliced bananas or diced mangoes.
Experiment with different types of nuts for added crunch and flavor.

73. Spinach and Feta Omelette

Servings: 1
Preparation time: 5 minutes
Cooking time: 7 minutes
Ingredients:
- 2 large eggs
- 1 cup fresh spinach leaves
- 1/4 cup crumbled feta cheese
- Salt and pepper to taste
- Cooking spray

Directions:
1. In a bowl, beat the eggs and season with salt and pepper.
2. Heat a non-stick skillet over medium heat and spray with cooking spray.
3. Add the spinach leaves to the skillet and cook until wilted, about 2 minutes.
4. Pour the beaten eggs over the spinach and sprinkle the feta cheese on top.
5. Cook until the eggs are set and the cheese has melted, about 5 minutes.
6. Gently fold the omelette in half and transfer to a plate.
7. Serve hot.

Nutritional Values per Serving: Sugar: 1g; Carbohydrates: 2g; Dietary Fiber: 1g; Total Fat: 15g; Saturated Fat: 6g; Unsaturated Fat: 7g; Cholesterol: 372mg; Sodium: 450mg; Phosphorus: 210mg; Potassium: 350mg

Difficulty Rating: ☆ ☆

Tips for Ingredient Variations:
Add diced tomatoes or sliced mushrooms for extra flavor and texture.
Substitute goat cheese for feta cheese for a tangy twist.

74. Overnight Chia Pudding

Servings: 1
Preparation time: 5 minutes
Cooking time: 0 minutes
Ingredients:
- 2 tablespoons chia seeds
- 1/2 cup unsweetened almond milk (or any milk of your choice)
- 1/4 teaspoon vanilla extract
- 1/4 cup fresh berries (e.g., blueberries, raspberries)
- 1 tablespoon chopped nuts (e.g., almonds, pecans)
- 1 teaspoon honey (optional)

Directions:
1. In a jar or bowl, combine the chia seeds, almond milk, and vanilla extract.
2. Stir well to ensure the chia seeds are fully immersed in the milk.
3. Cover the jar or bowl and refrigerate overnight or for at least 4 hours.
4. In the morning, give the chia pudding a good stir.
5. Top with fresh berries, chopped nuts, and drizzle with honey if desired.
6. Enjoy!

Nutritional Values per Serving: Sugar: 4g; Carbohydrates: 16g; Dietary Fiber: 11g; Total Fat: 12g; Saturated Fat: 1g; Unsaturated Fat: 10g; Cholesterol: 0mg; Sodium: 80mg; Phosphorus: 240mg; Potassium: 180mg

Difficulty Rating: ☆

Tips for Ingredient Variations:
Experiment with different flavors by adding cocoa powder or a dash of cinnamon to the chia pudding mixture.
Swap the almond milk for coconut milk for a tropical twist.

75. Whole Wheat Banana Pancakes

Servings: 2
Preparation time: 10 minutes
Cooking time: 5 minutes
Ingredients:
- 1 cup whole wheat flour
- 1 tablespoon baking powder
- 1/4 teaspoon salt
- 1 ripe banana, mashed
- 1 cup unsweetened almond milk (or any milk of your choice)
- 1 tablespoon honey (optional)
- Cooking spray or a small amount of oil for greasing the skillet

Directions:
1. In a large bowl, whisk together the whole wheat flour, baking powder, and salt.
2. In a separate bowl, combine the mashed banana, almond milk, and honey.
3. Pour the wet ingredients into the dry ingredients and stir until just combined.
4. Heat a non-stick skillet or griddle over medium heat and lightly grease with cooking spray or oil.
5. Pour 1/4 cup of batter onto the skillet for each pancake.
6. Cook until bubbles form on the surface, then flip and cook for another 1-2 minutes.
7. Repeat with the remaining batter.
8. Serve warm with your favorite toppings, such as sliced bananas or a drizzle of maple syrup.

Nutritional Values per Serving: Sugar: 7g; Carbohydrates: 38g; Dietary Fiber: 6g; Total Fat: 2g; Saturated Fat: 0g; Unsaturated Fat: 1g; Cholesterol: 0mg; Sodium: 320mg; Phosphorus: 280mg; Potassium: 330mg

Difficulty Rating: ☆☆

Tips for Ingredient Variations:
Add a handful of blueberries or chopped nuts to the pancake batter for extra flavor and texture.
Replace the honey with pureed dates for a natural sweetener alternative.

76. Veggie and Cheese Breakfast Quesadilla

Servings: 1
Preparation time: 5 minutes
Cooking time: 10 minutes
Ingredients:
- 2 small whole-wheat tortillas
- 1/4 cup shredded cheese (e.g., cheddar, mozzarella)
- 1/4 cup diced bell peppers (any color)
- 1/4 cup sliced mushrooms
- 2 tablespoons diced red onion
- Cooking spray or a small amount of oil for greasing the skillet

Directions:
1. Preheat a non-stick skillet over medium heat.
2. Place one tortilla in the skillet and sprinkle half of the shredded cheese on top.
3. Layer the diced bell peppers, sliced mushrooms, and diced red onion evenly over the cheese.
4. Sprinkle the remaining shredded cheese on top and cover with the second tortilla.
5. Cook for 3-4 minutes, or until the bottom tortilla is golden brown.
6. Carefully flip the quesadilla and cook for another 3-4 minutes, or until the cheese is melted and the second tortilla is golden brown.
7. Remove from the skillet and let it cool for a minute before cutting into wedges.
8. Serve warm.

Nutritional Values per Serving: Sugar: 3g; Carbohydrates: 40g; Dietary Fiber: 7g; Total Fat: 12g; Saturated Fat: 7g; Unsaturated Fat: 4g; Cholesterol: 35mg; Sodium: 420mg; Phosphorus: 320mg; Potassium: 480mg

Difficulty Rating: ☆☆

Tips for Ingredient Variations:
Add diced tomatoes or sliced zucchini for additional flavor and nutrients.
Use a different type of cheese, such as pepper jack or feta, for a unique taste.

77. Berry and Spinach Smoothie

Servings: 1
Preparation time: 5 minutes
Cooking time: 0 minutes
Ingredients:
- 1 cup fresh spinach leaves
- 1/2 cup frozen mixed berries (e.g., strawberries, blueberries, raspberries)
- 1/2 banana
- 1/2 cup unsweetened almond milk (or any milk of your choice)
- 1 tablespoon chia seeds (optional)
- 1 tablespoon honey (optional)

Directions:
1. Place the spinach leaves, frozen mixed berries, banana, almond milk, and chia seeds (if using) in a blender.
2. Blend until smooth and creamy.
3. Taste and add honey if desired for extra sweetness.
4. Pour into a glass and enjoy immediately.

Nutritional Values per Serving: Sugar: 14g; Carbohydrates: 36g; Dietary Fiber: 9g; Total Fat: 8g; Saturated Fat: 1g; Unsaturated Fat: 6g; Cholesterol: 0mg; Sodium: 150mg; Phosphorus: 230mg; Potassium: 760mg

Difficulty Rating: ☆
Tips for Ingredient Variations:
Add a scoop of protein powder for an extra protein boost.
Substitute kale or Swiss chard for spinach for a different flavor profile.

78. Smoked Salmon and Cream Cheese Bagel

Servings: 1
Preparation time: 5 minutes
Cooking time: 0 minutes
Ingredients:
- 1 whole wheat bagel, sliced and toasted
- 2 tablespoons cream cheese
- 2 ounces smoked salmon
- Sliced cucumber, red onion, and capers for garnish

Directions:
1. Spread the cream cheese evenly on both sides of the toasted bagel.
2. Layer the smoked salmon on one half of the bagel.
3. Top with sliced cucumber, red onion, and capers.
4. Place the other half of the bagel on top to form a sandwich.
5. Serve immediately.

Nutritional Values per Serving: Sugar: 3g; Carbohydrates: 48g; Dietary Fiber: 6g; Total Fat: 10g; Saturated Fat: 4g; Unsaturated Fat: 4g; Cholesterol: 15mg; Sodium: 600mg; Phosphorus: 240mg; Potassium: 420mg

Difficulty Rating: ☆
Tips for Ingredient Variations:
Use a flavored cream cheese, such as dill or chive, for added taste.
Substitute the whole wheat bagel with a gluten-free bagel if desired.

79. Avocado and Tomato Toast

Servings: 1
Preparation time: 5 minutes
Cooking time: 0 minutes
Ingredients:
- 1 slice whole grain bread, toasted
- 1/2 avocado, mashed
- 1 small tomato, sliced
- Salt and pepper to taste
- Fresh basil leaves for garnish (optional)

Directions:
1. Spread the mashed avocado evenly on the toasted bread.
2. Arrange the tomato slices on top of the avocado.
3. Season with salt and pepper to taste.
4. Optional: Garnish with fresh basil leaves.
5. Serve immediately.

Nutritional Values per Serving: Sugar: 2g; Carbohydrates: 17g; Dietary Fiber: 7g; Total Fat: 14g; Saturated Fat: 2g; Unsaturated Fat: 10g; Cholesterol: 0mg; Sodium: 150mg; Phosphorus: 200mg; Potassium: 500mg

Difficulty Rating: ☆

Tips for Ingredient Variations:
Add a sprinkle of red pepper flakes for a spicy kick.
Top with a poached egg for an extra protein boost.

80. Fruit and Nut Breakfast Quinoa

Servings: 2
Preparation time: 5 minutes
Cooking time: 10 minutes
Ingredients:
- 1 cup cooked quinoa
- 1/2 cup unsweetened almond milk (or any milk of your choice)
- 1/2 teaspoon vanilla extract
- 1/2 teaspoon cinnamon
- 1 tablespoon honey or maple syrup
- 1/4 cup chopped mixed nuts (e.g., almonds, walnuts)
- 1/4 cup dried cranberries or raisins
- 1/2 cup fresh berries (e.g., blueberries, raspberries)

Directions:
1. In a saucepan, combine the cooked quinoa, almond milk, vanilla extract, cinnamon, and honey or maple syrup.
2. Heat over medium heat, stirring occasionally, until heated through.
3. Remove from heat and stir in the chopped nuts, dried cranberries or raisins, and fresh berries.
4. Divide the mixture into bowls and serve warm.

Nutritional Values per Serving: Sugar: 16g; Carbohydrates: 55g; Dietary Fiber: 8g; Total Fat: 13g; Saturated Fat: 1g; Unsaturated Fat: 10g; Cholesterol: 0mg; Sodium: 50mg; Phosphorus: 300mg; Potassium: 480mg

Difficulty Rating: ☆ ☆

Tips for Ingredient Variations:
Add sliced bananas or diced apples for extra natural sweetness.
Sprinkle with a pinch of nutmeg or cardamom for a warm and aromatic flavor.

81. Grilled Chicken Caesar Salad

Servings: 2
Preparation time: 10 minutes
Cooking time: 5 minutes
Ingredients:
- 2 boneless, skinless chicken breasts
- 4 cups romaine lettuce, chopped
- 1/4 cup grated Parmesan cheese
- 1/4 cup Caesar dressing
- Croutons for garnish (optional)

Directions:
1. Preheat the grill to medium-high heat.
2. Season the chicken breasts with salt and pepper.
3. Grill the chicken for 4-5 minutes on each side until cooked through.
4. Let the chicken rest for a few minutes, then slice it into thin strips.
5. In a large bowl, toss the romaine lettuce with the Caesar dressing.
6. Add the sliced chicken and grated Parmesan cheese to the bowl and toss gently to combine.
7. Serve the salad with croutons on top, if desired.

Nutritional Values per Serving: Sugar: 2g; Carbohydrates: 7g; Dietary Fiber: 3g; Total Fat: 10g; Saturated Fat: 3g; Unsaturated Fat: 6g; Cholesterol: 60mg; Sodium: 400mg; Phosphorus: 200mg; Potassium: 400mg

Difficulty Rating: ★★☆☆☆

Tips for Ingredient Variations:
For a vegetarian option, substitute the chicken with grilled tofu or chickpeas.
Add cherry tomatoes or avocado slices for extra flavor and texture.

82. Quinoa and Vegetable Stir-Fry

Servings: 4
Preparation time: 5 minutes
Cooking time: 10 minutes
Ingredients:
- 1 cup quinoa, cooked
- 1 tablespoon olive oil
- 1 onion, thinly sliced
- 2 bell peppers, thinly sliced
- 1 zucchini, sliced
- 1 cup broccoli florets
- 2 cloves garlic, minced
- 2 tablespoons low-sodium soy sauce
- 1 tablespoon sesame oil
- Sesame seeds for garnish (optional)

Directions:
1. Heat the olive oil in a large skillet over medium heat.
2. Add the onion, bell peppers, zucchini, and broccoli to the skillet.
3. Stir-fry the vegetables for 5-6 minutes until they are tender-crisp.
4. Add the minced garlic to the skillet and cook for an additional minute.
5. Stir in the cooked quinoa, soy sauce, and sesame oil.
6. Cook for another 2-3 minutes, stirring occasionally.
7. Serve the stir-fry hot, garnished with sesame seeds if desired.

Nutritional Values per Serving: Sugar: 4g; Carbohydrates: 30g; Dietary Fiber: 6g; Total Fat: 8g; Saturated Fat: 1g; Unsaturated Fat: 7g; Cholesterol: 0mg; Sodium: 300mg; Phosphorus: 150mg; Potassium: 600mg

Difficulty Rating: ★★☆☆☆

Tips for Ingredient Variations:
Feel free to add your favorite vegetables such as snap peas or mushrooms.
For added protein, toss in some cooked shrimp or tofu cubes.

83. Turkey and Avocado Wrap

Servings: 2
Preparation time: 10 minutes
Cooking time: 5 minutes
Ingredients:

- 4 whole wheat tortillas
- 8 slices turkey breast
- 1 avocado, sliced
- 4 lettuce leaves
- 2 tablespoons Greek yogurt
- 1 tablespoon Dijon mustard

Directions:

1. Lay out the tortillas on a clean surface.
2. Spread Greek yogurt and Dijon mustard evenly on each tortilla.
3. Place two slices of turkey breast on each tortilla.
4. Top with avocado slices and a lettuce leaf.
5. Roll up the tortillas tightly, tucking in the sides as you go.
6. Slice the wraps in half and serve.

Nutritional Values per Serving: Sugar: 2g; Carbohydrates: 25g; Dietary Fiber: 6g; Total Fat: 10g; Saturated Fat: 2g; Unsaturated Fat: 8g; Cholesterol: 25mg; Sodium: 400mg; Phosphorus: 150mg; Potassium: 400mg

Difficulty Rating: ★☆☆☆

Tips for Ingredient Variations:

Experiment with different types of deli meats like roast beef or chicken.

Add a slice of cheese or a sprinkle of herbs for extra flavor.

84. Caprese Pasta Salad

Servings: 4
Preparation time: 5 minutes
Cooking time: 10 minutes
Ingredients:

- 8 ounces whole wheat penne pasta
- 1 cup cherry tomatoes, halved
- 1 cup fresh mozzarella balls
- 1/4 cup fresh basil leaves, torn
- 2 tablespoons balsamic vinegar
- 1 tablespoon olive oil
- Salt and pepper to taste

Directions:

1. Cook the penne pasta according to package instructions.
2. Drain the cooked pasta and rinse with cold water.
3. In a large bowl, combine the pasta, cherry tomatoes, mozzarella balls, and torn basil leaves.
4. In a small bowl, whisk together the balsamic vinegar, olive oil, salt, and pepper.
5. Pour the dressing over the pasta salad and toss gently to combine.
6. Serve the salad chilled or at room temperature.

Nutritional Values per Serving: Sugar: 3g; Carbohydrates: 35g; Dietary Fiber: 6g; Total Fat: 10g; Saturated Fat: 4g; Unsaturated Fat: 6g; Cholesterol: 10mg; Sodium: 200mg; Phosphorus: 200mg; Potassium: 300mg

Difficulty Rating: ★☆☆☆

Tips for Ingredient Variations:

Try using different types of pasta like fusilli or farfalle for a fun twist.

Add some pine nuts or black olives for extra texture and flavor.

85. Salmon and Asparagus Foil Pack

Servings: 2
Preparation time: 5 minutes
Cooking time: 10 minutes
Ingredients:
- 2 salmon fillets
- 1 bunch asparagus, trimmed
- 2 tablespoons lemon juice
- 2 tablespoons olive oil
- 2 cloves garlic, minced
- Salt and pepper to taste

Directions:
1. Preheat the oven to 400°F (200°C).
2. Place each salmon fillet on a piece of aluminum foil.
3. Arrange the asparagus around the salmon.
4. In a small bowl, whisk together the lemon juice, olive oil, minced garlic, salt, and pepper.
5. Drizzle the mixture over the salmon and asparagus.
6. Fold the foil to create a packet, sealing it tightly.
7. Place the foil packets on a baking sheet and bake for 10 minutes.
8. Carefully open the packets and serve hot.

Nutritional Values per Serving: Sugar: 1g; Carbohydrates: 5g; Dietary Fiber: 2g; Total Fat: 20g; Saturated Fat: 3g; Unsaturated Fat: 17g; Cholesterol: 50mg; Sodium: 200mg; Phosphorus: 300mg; Potassium: 600mg

Difficulty Rating: ★★☆☆

Tips for Ingredient Variations:
Swap the salmon for trout or tilapia if you prefer a different fish.
Add some lemon slices or dill for a burst of freshness.

86. Greek Chicken Pita

Servings: 2
Preparation time: 10 minutes
Cooking time: 5 minutes
Ingredients:
- 2 boneless, skinless chicken breasts
- 2 whole wheat pita breads
- 1/4 cup Greek yogurt
- 1/4 cup cucumber, diced
- 1/4 cup cherry tomatoes, halved
- 2 tablespoons red onion, thinly sliced
- 2 tablespoons fresh dill, chopped
- Juice of 1/2 lemon
- Salt and pepper to taste

Directions:
1. Season the chicken breasts with salt and pepper.
2. Grill or pan-fry the chicken for 4-5 minutes on each side until cooked through.
3. Let the chicken rest for a few minutes, then slice it into thin strips.
4. In a small bowl, combine the Greek yogurt, diced cucumber, cherry tomatoes, red onion, fresh dill, lemon juice, salt, and pepper.
5. Warm the pita breads in a toaster or oven.
6. Spread the Greek yogurt mixture inside each pita bread.
7. Fill the pitas with the sliced chicken and serve.

Nutritional Values per Serving: Sugar: 3g; Carbohydrates: 30g; Dietary Fiber: 6g; Total Fat: 5g; Saturated Fat: 1g; Unsaturated Fat: 4g; Cholesterol: 75mg; Sodium: 300mg; Phosphorus: 200mg; Potassium: 400mg

Difficulty Rating: ★★☆☆

Tips for Ingredient Variations:
Add some Kalamata olives or feta cheese for a traditional Greek twist.
Include some sliced bell peppers or lettuce for added crunch.

87. Egg Salad Lettuce Wraps

Servings: 2
Preparation time: 10 minutes
Cooking time: 5 minutes
Ingredients:
- 4 hard-boiled eggs, chopped
- 2 tablespoons Greek yogurt
- 1 tablespoon Dijon mustard
- 2 tablespoons green onions, chopped
- Salt and pepper to taste
- 4 large lettuce leaves

Directions:
1. In a bowl, combine the chopped hard-boiled eggs, Greek yogurt, Dijon mustard, green onions, salt, and pepper.
2. Mix well until all ingredients are evenly incorporated.
3. Lay out the lettuce leaves on a clean surface.
4. Spoon the egg salad mixture onto each lettuce leaf.
5. Roll up the lettuce leaves, securing them with toothpicks if needed.
6. Serve the lettuce wraps chilled or at room temperature.

Nutritional Values per Serving: Sugar: 2g; Carbohydrates: 5g; Dietary Fiber: 2g; Total Fat: 15g; Saturated Fat: 4g; Unsaturated Fat: 11g; Cholesterol: 330mg; Sodium: 200mg; Phosphorus: 300mg; Potassium: 300mg

Difficulty Rating: ★☆☆☆☆

Tips for Ingredient Variations:

Add some diced celery or bell peppers for extra crunch and flavor.

Sprinkle some paprika or cayenne pepper for a touch of spice.

88. Veggie and Hummus Wrap

Servings: 2
Preparation time: 10 minutes
Cooking time: 5 minutes
Ingredients:
- 2 whole wheat tortillas
- 1/2 cup hummus
- 1/2 cup baby spinach leaves
- 1/2 cup shredded carrots
- 1/2 cup sliced cucumbers
- 1/4 cup sliced red bell peppers
- 1/4 cup sliced yellow bell peppers

Directions:
1. Lay out the tortillas on a clean surface.
2. Spread hummus evenly on each tortilla.
3. Layer the baby spinach leaves, shredded carrots, sliced cucumbers, red bell peppers, and yellow bell peppers on top of the hummus.
4. Roll up the tortillas tightly, tucking in the sides as you go.
5. Slice the wraps in half and serve.

Nutritional Values per Serving: Sugar: 4g; Carbohydrates: 30g; Dietary Fiber: 6g; Total Fat: 10g; Saturated Fat: 2g; Unsaturated Fat: 8g; Cholesterol: 0mg; Sodium: 400mg; Phosphorus: 150mg; Potassium: 400mg

Difficulty Rating: ★☆☆☆☆

Tips for Ingredient Variations:

Experiment with different flavors of hummus like roasted red pepper or garlic.

Add some sliced avocado or sprouts for extra creaminess and texture.

89. Tuna and White Bean Salad

Servings: 2
Preparation time: 10 minutes
Cooking time: 5 minutes
Ingredients:
- 1 can tuna, drained
- 1 can white beans, rinsed and drained
- 1/4 cup red onion, finely chopped
- 1/4 cup fresh parsley, chopped
- 2 tablespoons lemon juice
- 2 tablespoons olive oil
- Salt and pepper to taste

Directions:

1. In a bowl, combine the drained tuna, white beans, red onion, fresh parsley, lemon juice, olive oil, salt, and pepper.
2. Mix well until all ingredients are evenly incorporated.
3. Serve the tuna and white bean salad chilled or at room temperature.

Nutritional Values per Serving: Sugar: 1g; Carbohydrates: 20g; Dietary Fiber: 5g; Total Fat: 10g; Saturated Fat: 1g; Unsaturated Fat: 9g; Cholesterol: 15mg; Sodium: 200mg; Phosphorus: 200mg; Potassium: 400mg

Difficulty Rating: ★☆☆☆☆

Tips for Ingredient Variations:

Add some diced tomatoes or cucumbers for extra freshness and crunch.

Sprinkle some feta cheese or olives for a Mediterranean twist.

90. Veggie Omelette

Servings: 2
Preparation time: 5 minutes
Cooking time: 10 minutes
Ingredients:
- 4 large eggs
- 1/4 cup milk
- 1/2 cup diced bell peppers (any color)
- 1/2 cup sliced mushrooms
- 1/4 cup diced onions
- 1/4 cup shredded cheddar cheese
- Salt and pepper to taste
- Cooking spray or olive oil for the pan

Directions:

1. In a bowl, whisk together the eggs, milk, salt, and pepper.
2. Heat a non-stick skillet over medium heat and coat it with cooking spray or olive oil.
3. Add the diced bell peppers, sliced mushrooms, and diced onions to the skillet.
4. Cook the vegetables for 3-4 minutes until they are tender.
5. Pour the egg mixture over the cooked vegetables in the skillet.
6. Sprinkle the shredded cheddar cheese on top.
7. Cook the omelette for 3-4 minutes until the eggs are set.
8. Carefully fold the omelette in half and transfer it to a plate.
9. Slice the omelette and serve hot.

Nutritional Values per Serving: Sugar: 2g; Carbohydrates: 10g; Dietary Fiber: 2g; Total Fat: 15g; Saturated Fat: 6g; Unsaturated Fat: 9g; Cholesterol: 370mg; Sodium: 300mg; Phosphorus: 300mg; Potassium: 400mg

Difficulty Rating: ★★☆☆☆

Tips for Ingredient Variations:

Customize your omelette by adding your favorite vegetables like spinach or tomatoes.

Experiment with different types of cheese such as feta or goat cheese for unique flavors.

91. Grilled Salmon with Lemon and Dill

Servings: 2
Preparation time: 5 minutes
Cooking time: 10 minutes
Ingredients:
- 2 salmon fillets
- 1 lemon, sliced
- Fresh dill, chopped
- Salt and pepper to taste

Directions:
1. Preheat the grill to medium-high heat.
2. Season the salmon fillets with salt and pepper.
3. Place the lemon slices on top of the salmon.
4. Sprinkle the chopped dill over the salmon.
5. Grill the salmon for about 5 minutes on each side, or until cooked through.
6. Serve hot with a side of steamed vegetables or a salad.

Nutritional Values per Serving: Sugar: 0g; Carbohydrates: 0g; Dietary Fiber: 0g; Total Fat: 15g; Saturated Fat: 2g; Unsaturated Fat: 13g; Cholesterol: 47mg; Sodium: 63mg; Phosphorus: 235mg; Potassium: 534mg

Difficulty Rating: ☆☆
Tips for Ingredient Variations:
Substitute dill with other fresh herbs like parsley or basil.
Add a sprinkle of paprika for a touch of smoky flavor.

92. Grilled Chicken with Balsamic Glaze

Servings: 4
Preparation time: 5 minutes
Cooking time: 10 minutes
Ingredients:
- 4 boneless, skinless chicken breasts
- 1/4 cup balsamic vinegar
- 1 tablespoon olive oil
- Salt and pepper to taste

Directions:
1. Preheat the grill to medium-high heat.
2. Season the chicken breasts with salt and pepper.
3. In a small bowl, whisk together the balsamic vinegar and olive oil.
4. Brush the balsamic glaze onto both sides of the chicken breasts.
5. Grill the chicken for about 5 minutes on each side, or until cooked through.
6. Serve hot with a side of roasted vegetables or quinoa.

Nutritional Values per Serving: Sugar: 2g; Carbohydrates: 2g; Dietary Fiber: 0g; Total Fat: 3g; Saturated Fat: 0g; Unsaturated Fat: 3g; Cholesterol: 68mg; Sodium: 86mg; Phosphorus: 217mg; Potassium: 381mg

Difficulty Rating: ☆☆☆
Tips for Ingredient Variations:
Use different types of vinegar such as apple cider or red wine vinegar.
Add a sprinkle of dried herbs like thyme or rosemary for extra flavor.

93. Shrimp Stir-Fry with Vegetables

Servings: 2
Preparation time: 5 minutes
Cooking time: 10 minutes
Ingredients:
- 8 ounces shrimp, peeled and deveined
- 1 cup mixed vegetables (bell peppers, broccoli, snap peas)
- 2 cloves garlic, minced
- 1 tablespoon low-sodium soy sauce
- 1 tablespoon sesame oil
- Salt and pepper to taste

Directions:
1. Heat the sesame oil in a large skillet or wok over medium-high heat.
2. Add the minced garlic and stir-fry for 1 minute.
3. Add the shrimp and mixed vegetables to the skillet.
4. Stir-fry for about 5 minutes, or until the shrimp is cooked and the vegetables are tender-crisp.
5. Drizzle the soy sauce over the stir-fry and season with salt and pepper.
6. Serve hot with a side of brown rice or cauliflower rice.

Nutritional Values per Serving: Sugar: 3g; Carbohydrates: 9g; Dietary Fiber: 3g; Total Fat: 7g; Saturated Fat: 1g; Unsaturated Fat: 6g; Cholesterol: 143mg; Sodium: 430mg; Phosphorus: 241mg; Potassium: 397mg

Difficulty Rating: ☆☆☆

Tips for Ingredient Variations:
Add sliced mushrooms or water chestnuts for added texture.
Use tamari sauce instead of soy sauce for a gluten-free option.

94. Beef and Broccoli Stir-Fry

Servings: 4
Preparation time: 5 minutes
Cooking time: 10 minutes
Ingredients:
- 1 pound beef sirloin, thinly sliced
- 2 cups broccoli florets
- 1/4 cup low-sodium soy sauce
- 2 tablespoons oyster sauce
- 1 tablespoon cornstarch
- 1 tablespoon vegetable oil
- Salt and pepper to taste

Directions:
1. In a small bowl, whisk together the soy sauce, oyster sauce, and cornstarch.
2. Heat the vegetable oil in a large skillet or wok over medium-high heat.
3. Add the beef slices and stir-fry for about 3 minutes, or until browned.
4. Add the broccoli florets to the skillet and stir-fry for another 3 minutes.
5. Pour the sauce mixture over the beef and broccoli.
6. Stir-fry for 1-2 minutes, or until the sauce thickens and coats the beef and broccoli.
7. Season with salt and pepper to taste.
8. Serve hot with a side of steamed brown rice or quinoa.

Nutritional Values per Serving: Sugar: 2g; Carbohydrates: 9g; Dietary Fiber: 2g; Total Fat: 8g; Saturated Fat: 2g; Unsaturated Fat: 6g; Cholesterol: 70mg; Sodium: 671mg; Phosphorus: 209mg; Potassium: 527mg

Difficulty Rating: ☆☆☆☆

Tips for Ingredient Variations:
Substitute beef with chicken or tofu for a different protein option.
Add sliced carrots or bell peppers for extra color and flavor.

95. Mediterranean Tuna Salad

Servings: 2
Preparation time: 5 minutes
Cooking time: 0 minutes
Ingredients:
- 2 cans tuna in water, drained
- 1/4 cup diced cucumber
- 1/4 cup diced tomatoes
- 1/4 cup diced red onion
- 2 tablespoons chopped Kalamata olives
- 2 tablespoons feta cheese, crumbled
- 1 tablespoon extra virgin olive oil
- 1 tablespoon lemon juice
- Salt and pepper to taste

Directions:
1. In a large bowl, combine the tuna, cucumber, tomatoes, red onion, Kalamata olives, and feta cheese.
2. Drizzle the olive oil and lemon juice over the mixture.
3. Season with salt and pepper to taste.
4. Toss everything together until well combined.
5. Serve chilled on a bed of mixed greens or whole wheat pita bread.

Nutritional Values per Serving: Sugar: 2g; Carbohydrates: 7g; Dietary Fiber: 2g; Total Fat: 12g; Saturated Fat: 3g; Unsaturated Fat: 9g; Cholesterol: 37mg; Sodium: 602mg; Phosphorus: 167mg; Potassium: 328mg

Difficulty Rating: ☆ ☆

Tips for Ingredient Variations:
Add chopped fresh herbs like parsley or basil for extra freshness.
Substitute feta cheese with goat cheese or mozzarella.

96. Veggie Omelette

Servings: 1
Preparation time: 5 minutes
Cooking time: 5 minutes
Ingredients:
- 2 eggs
- 1/4 cup diced bell peppers
- 1/4 cup diced tomatoes
- 1/4 cup chopped spinach
- 2 tablespoons diced onion
- 1 tablespoon olive oil
- Salt and pepper to taste

Directions:
1. In a small bowl, whisk the eggs until well beaten.
2. Heat the olive oil in a non-stick skillet over medium heat.
3. Add the diced bell peppers, tomatoes, spinach, and onion to the skillet.
4. Sauté the vegetables for 2-3 minutes, or until slightly softened.
5. Pour the beaten eggs over the vegetables in the skillet.
6. Season with salt and pepper to taste.
7. Cook the omelette for 2-3 minutes, or until the eggs are set.
8. Carefully fold the omelette in half and slide onto a plate.

Nutritional Values per Serving: Sugar: 4g; Carbohydrates: 9g; Dietary Fiber: 3g; Total Fat: 15g; Saturated Fat: 4g; Unsaturated Fat: 11g; Cholesterol: 372mg; Sodium: 169mg; Phosphorus: 226mg; Potassium: 487mg

Difficulty Rating: ☆ ☆

Tips for Ingredient Variations:
Add diced mushrooms or zucchini for extra texture.
Sprinkle grated cheese on top of the omelette before folding.

97. Quinoa Salad with Roasted Vegetables

Servings: 4
Preparation time: 5 minutes
Cooking time: 10 minutes
Ingredients:
- 1 cup cooked quinoa
- 1 cup mixed roasted vegetables (bell peppers, zucchini, eggplant)
- 1/4 cup crumbled feta cheese
- 2 tablespoons chopped fresh parsley
- 2 tablespoons lemon juice
- 1 tablespoon extra virgin olive oil
- Salt and pepper to taste

Directions:
1. In a large bowl, combine the cooked quinoa, roasted vegetables, feta cheese, and parsley.
2. Drizzle the lemon juice and olive oil over the mixture.
3. Season with salt and pepper to taste.
4. Toss everything together until well combined.
5. Serve chilled as a light main dish or a side dish.
6. **Nutritional Values per Serving:** Sugar: 2g; Carbohydrates: 22g; Dietary Fiber: 4g; Total Fat: 7g; Saturated Fat: 2g; Unsaturated Fat: 5g; Cholesterol: 8mg; Sodium: 136mg; Phosphorus: 143mg; Potassium: 355mg

Difficulty Rating: ☆☆
Tips for Ingredient Variations:
Add roasted cherry tomatoes or asparagus for extra flavor.
Substitute feta cheese with goat cheese or Parmesan.

98. Caprese Stuffed Chicken Breast

Servings: 2
Preparation time: 5 minutes
Cooking time: 10 minutes
Ingredients:
- 2 boneless, skinless chicken breasts
- 2 slices mozzarella cheese
- 4 slices tomato
- Fresh basil leaves
- Salt and pepper to taste

Directions:
1. Preheat the oven to 400°F (200°C).
2. Cut a slit in each chicken breast to create a pocket.
3. Season the chicken breasts with salt and pepper.
4. Stuff each chicken breast with a slice of mozzarella cheese, tomato slices, and fresh basil leaves.
5. Secure the chicken breasts with toothpicks to hold the stuffing in place.
6. Place the stuffed chicken breasts on a baking sheet.
7. Bake for 10 minutes, or until the chicken is cooked through and the cheese is melted.
8. Remove the toothpicks before serving.

Nutritional Values per Serving: Sugar: 2g; Carbohydrates: 2g; Dietary Fiber: 0g; Total Fat: 9g; Saturated Fat: 4g; Unsaturated Fat: 5g; Cholesterol: 84mg; Sodium: 245mg; Phosphorus: 204mg; Potassium: 332mg

Difficulty Rating: ☆☆☆
Tips for Ingredient Variations:
Use other types of cheese like provolone or Swiss.
Add a drizzle of balsamic glaze over the stuffed chicken breasts before serving.

99. Spinach and Mushroom Frittata

Servings: 4
Preparation time: 5 minutes
Cooking time: 10 minutes
Ingredients:
- 6 eggs
- 1 cup fresh spinach leaves
- 1 cup sliced mushrooms
- 1/4 cup diced onion
- 2 tablespoons grated Parmesan cheese
- 1 tablespoon olive oil
- Salt and pepper to taste

Directions:
1. In a large bowl, whisk the eggs until well beaten.
2. Heat the olive oil in a non-stick skillet over medium heat.
3. Add the diced onion and sliced mushrooms to the skillet.
4. Sauté the vegetables for 2-3 minutes, or until slightly softened.
5. Add the fresh spinach leaves to the skillet and cook until wilted.
6. Pour the beaten eggs over the vegetables in the skillet.
7. Season with salt and pepper to taste.
8. Cook the frittata for 5-7 minutes, or until the eggs are set.
9. Sprinkle the grated Parmesan cheese over the frittata.

Nutritional Values per Serving: Sugar: 1g; Carbohydrates: 3g; Dietary Fiber: 1g; Total Fat: 10g; Saturated Fat: 3g; Unsaturated Fat: 7g; Cholesterol: 186mg; Sodium: 149mg; Phosphorus: 143mg; Potassium: 324mg

Difficulty Rating: ☆ ☆

Tips for Ingredient Variations: Add diced bell peppers or sun-dried tomatoes for extra flavor. Sprinkle chopped fresh herbs like thyme or chives on top before serving.

100. Black Bean and Corn Salad

Servings: 4
Preparation time: 5 minutes
Cooking time: 0 minutes
Ingredients:
- 1 can black beans, rinsed and drained
- 1 cup frozen corn, thawed
- 1/4 cup diced red bell pepper
- 1/4 cup diced red onion
- 2 tablespoons chopped fresh cilantro
- 2 tablespoons lime juice
- 1 tablespoon extra virgin olive oil
- Salt and pepper to taste

Directions:
1. In a large bowl, combine the black beans, corn, red bell pepper, red onion, and cilantro.
2. Drizzle the lime juice and olive oil over the mixture.
3. Season with salt and pepper to taste.
4. Toss everything together until well combined.
5. Serve chilled as a side dish or as a topping for tacos or grilled chicken.

Nutritional Values per Serving: Sugar: 2g; Carbohydrates: 23g; Dietary Fiber: 6g; Total Fat: 6g; Saturated Fat: 1g; Unsaturated Fat: 5g; Cholesterol: 0mg; Sodium: 7mg; Phosphorus: 138mg; Potassium: 444mg

Difficulty Rating: ☆ ☆

Tips for Ingredient Variations:
Add diced avocado or jalapeño for extra creaminess or spiciness.
Substitute cilantro with parsley or mint if preferred.

101. Avocado and Tomato Salad

Servings: 2
Preparation time: 10 minutes
Cooking time: 5 minutes
Ingredients:
- 1 ripe avocado, diced
- 1 medium tomato, diced
- 1 tablespoon lemon juice
- 1 tablespoon olive oil
- Salt and pepper to taste

Directions:
1. In a bowl, combine the diced avocado and tomato.
2. Drizzle lemon juice and olive oil over the mixture.
3. Season with salt and pepper to taste.
4. Toss gently to combine.

Nutritional Values per Serving: Sugar: 0g; Carbohydrates: 7g; Dietary Fiber: 5g; Total Fat: 15g; Saturated Fat: 2g; Unsaturated Fat: 11g; Cholesterol: 0mg; Sodium: 5mg; Phosphorus: 45mg; Potassium: 487mg

Difficulty Rating: ☆ ☆

Tips for Ingredient Variations:
Add diced cucumber for extra crunch.
Sprinkle with chopped fresh herbs like cilantro or basil for added flavor.

102. Greek Yogurt with Berries

Servings: 1
Preparation time: 5 minutes
Cooking time: 0 minutes
Ingredients:
- 1/2 cup plain Greek yogurt
- 1/4 cup mixed berries (such as blueberries, strawberries, and raspberries)
- 1 tablespoon chopped nuts (such as almonds or walnuts)
- 1 teaspoon honey (optional)

Directions:
1. In a bowl, spoon the Greek yogurt.
2. Top with mixed berries and chopped nuts.
3. Drizzle with honey if desired.

Nutritional Values per Serving: Sugar: 5g; Carbohydrates: 11g; Dietary Fiber: 2g; Total Fat: 10g; Saturated Fat: 1g; Unsaturated Fat: 8g; Cholesterol: 5mg; Sodium: 30mg; Phosphorus: 150mg; Potassium: 180mg

Difficulty Rating: ☆

Tips for Ingredient Variations:
Use flavored Greek yogurt for added variety.
Substitute the nuts with granola for a different texture.

103. Veggie Wrap

Servings: 1
Preparation time: 10 minutes
Cooking time: 5 minutes
Ingredients:
- 1 whole wheat tortilla
- 1/4 cup hummus
- 1/4 cup sliced cucumbers
- 1/4 cup sliced bell peppers
- 1/4 cup shredded carrots
- 1/4 cup baby spinach leaves

Directions:
1. Spread hummus evenly on the whole wheat tortilla.
2. Layer the sliced cucumbers, bell peppers, shredded carrots, and baby spinach leaves on top.
3. Roll the tortilla tightly.

Nutritional Values per Serving: Sugar: 2g; Carbohydrates: 30g; Dietary Fiber: 7g; Total Fat: 6g; Saturated Fat: 1g; Unsaturated Fat: 3g; Cholesterol: 0mg; Sodium: 350mg; Phosphorus: 100mg; Potassium: 400mg

Difficulty Rating: ☆☆

Tips for Ingredient Variations:
Add sliced avocado for extra creaminess.
Substitute the hummus with low-fat cream cheese for a different flavor.

104. Tuna Salad Lettuce Wraps

Servings: 2
Preparation time: 10 minutes
Cooking time: 0 minutes
Ingredients:
- 1 can tuna, drained
- 2 tablespoons mayonnaise
- 1 tablespoon Dijon mustard
- 1/4 cup diced celery
- 1/4 cup diced red onion
- Salt and pepper to taste
- 4 large lettuce leaves

Directions:
1. In a bowl, combine the tuna, mayonnaise, Dijon mustard, diced celery, and diced red onion.
2. Season with salt and pepper to taste.
3. Spoon the tuna salad onto the lettuce leaves.
4. Roll up the lettuce leaves to form wraps.

Nutritional Values per Serving: Sugar: 1g; Carbohydrates: 4g; Dietary Fiber: 1g; Total Fat: 14g; Saturated Fat: 2g; Unsaturated Fat: 10g; Cholesterol: 25mg; Sodium: 350mg; Phosphorus: 150mg; Potassium: 250mg

Difficulty Rating: ☆☆

Tips for Ingredient Variations:
Add diced pickles or olives for extra flavor.
Substitute the lettuce leaves with whole wheat wraps for a heartier snack.

105. Caprese Skewers

Servings: 2
Preparation time: 10 minutes
Cooking time: 0 minutes
Ingredients:
- 8 cherry tomatoes
- 8 small mozzarella balls
- 8 fresh basil leaves
- 1 tablespoon balsamic glaze
- Salt and pepper to taste

Directions:
1. Thread a cherry tomato, mozzarella ball, and basil leaf onto a skewer.
2. Repeat with the remaining ingredients.
3. Drizzle with balsamic glaze.
4. Season with salt and pepper to taste.

Nutritional Values per Serving: Sugar: 4g; Carbohydrates: 5g; Dietary Fiber: 1g; Total Fat: 12g; Saturated Fat: 6g; Unsaturated Fat: 5g; Cholesterol: 30mg; Sodium: 180mg; Phosphorus: 200mg; Potassium: 200mg

Difficulty Rating: ☆

Tips for Ingredient Variations:
Add a drizzle of pesto for added flavor.
Use different types of cheese, such as feta or goat cheese, for variety.

106. Apple and Almond Butter Slices

Servings: 1
Preparation time: 5 minutes
Cooking time: 0 minutes
Ingredients:
- 1 apple, sliced
- 2 tablespoons almond butter
- 1 tablespoon chopped almonds
- Cinnamon (optional)

Directions:
1. Arrange the apple slices on a plate.
2. Spread almond butter on each slice.
3. Sprinkle chopped almonds on top.
4. Sprinkle with cinnamon if desired.

Nutritional Values per Serving: Sugar: 12g; Carbohydrates: 20g; Dietary Fiber: 5g; Total Fat: 14g; Saturated Fat: 1g; Unsaturated Fat: 11g; Cholesterol: 0mg; Sodium: 0mg; Phosphorus: 100mg; Potassium: 200mg

Difficulty Rating: ☆

Tips for Ingredient Variations:
Use peanut butter or cashew butter instead of almond butter.
Sprinkle with shredded coconut for added texture.

107. Cucumber and Cream Cheese Bites

Servings: 2
Preparation time: 10 minutes
Cooking time: 0 minutes
Ingredients:
- 1 cucumber, sliced
- 4 tablespoons cream cheese
- 2 tablespoons chopped fresh dill
- Salt and pepper to taste

Directions:
1. Spread cream cheese evenly on each cucumber slice.
2. Sprinkle chopped fresh dill on top.
3. Season with salt and pepper to taste.

Nutritional Values per Serving: Sugar: 2g; Carbohydrates: 5g; Dietary Fiber: 1g; Total Fat: 12g; Saturated Fat: 7g; Unsaturated Fat: 3g; Cholesterol: 40mg; Sodium: 80mg; Phosphorus: 80mg; Potassium: 200mg

Difficulty Rating: ☆

Tips for Ingredient Variations:
Add a slice of smoked salmon or turkey for extra protein.
Substitute the cream cheese with goat cheese for a tangier flavor.

108. Edamame Salad

Servings: 2
Preparation time: 10 minutes
Cooking time: 0 minutes
Ingredients:
- 1 cup shelled edamame, cooked
- 1/4 cup diced red bell pepper
- 1/4 cup diced cucumber
- 2 tablespoons chopped fresh cilantro
- 1 tablespoon rice vinegar
- 1 tablespoon low-sodium soy sauce
- 1 teaspoon sesame oil
- 1/2 teaspoon grated ginger

Directions:
1. In a bowl, combine the cooked edamame, diced red bell pepper, diced cucumber, and chopped fresh cilantro.
2. In a separate small bowl, whisk together the rice vinegar, low-sodium soy sauce, sesame oil, and grated ginger.
3. Pour the dressing over the edamame mixture.
4. Toss gently to combine.

Nutritional Values per Serving: Sugar: 2g; Carbohydrates: 10g; Dietary Fiber: 4g; Total Fat: 6g; Saturated Fat: 1g; Unsaturated Fat: 4g; Cholesterol: 0mg; Sodium: 150mg; Phosphorus: 100mg; Potassium: 300mg

Difficulty Rating: ☆ ☆

Tips for Ingredient Variations:
Add diced avocado for extra creaminess.
Sprinkle with sesame seeds for added texture.

109. Roasted Chickpeas

Servings: 2
Preparation time: 5 minutes
Cooking time: 10 minutes
Ingredients:
- 1 can chickpeas, drained and rinsed
- 1 tablespoon olive oil
- 1 teaspoon smoked paprika
- 1/2 teaspoon garlic powder
- 1/2 teaspoon cumin
- Salt and pepper to taste

Directions:
1. Preheat the oven to 400°F (200°C).
2. In a bowl, toss the chickpeas with olive oil, smoked paprika, garlic powder, cumin, salt, and pepper.
3. Spread the seasoned chickpeas on a baking sheet.
4. Roast in the preheated oven for 10 minutes, or until crispy.

Nutritional Values per Serving: Sugar: 2g; Carbohydrates: 22g; Dietary Fiber: 6g; Total Fat: 7g; Saturated Fat: 1g; Unsaturated Fat: 5g; Cholesterol: 0mg; Sodium: 330mg; Phosphorus: 100mg; Potassium: 300mg

Difficulty Rating: ☆ ☆

Tips for Ingredient Variations:
Add a sprinkle of chili powder for a spicy kick. Experiment with different spice blends, such as curry or Cajun seasoning.

110. Berry Smoothie

Servings: 1
Preparation time: 5 minutes
Cooking time: 0 minutes
Ingredients:
- 1/2 cup frozen mixed berries
- 1/2 cup unsweetened almond milk
- 1/4 cup plain Greek yogurt
- 1 tablespoon chia seeds
- 1 teaspoon honey (optional)

Directions:
1. In a blender, combine the frozen mixed berries, almond milk, Greek yogurt, chia seeds, and honey if desired.
2. Blend until smooth and creamy.

Nutritional Values per Serving: Sugar: 9g; Carbohydrates: 18g; Dietary Fiber: 7g; Total Fat: 8g; Saturated Fat: 1g; Unsaturated Fat: 6g; Cholesterol: 5mg; Sodium: 80mg; Phosphorus: 200mg; Potassium: 200mg

Difficulty Rating: ☆

Tips for Ingredient Variations:
Add a handful of spinach for an extra nutrient boost.
Substitute almond milk with coconut milk for a different flavor.

111. Chocolate Banana Pudding

Servings: 4
Preparation time: 5 minutes
Cooking time: 10 minutes
Ingredients:
- 2 ripe bananas, mashed
- 1/4 cup unsweetened cocoa powder
- 1/2 cup low-fat milk
- 1 teaspoon vanilla extract
- 1 tablespoon honey (optional)

Directions:
1. In a saucepan, combine mashed bananas, cocoa powder, milk, and vanilla extract.
2. Cook over medium heat, stirring constantly until the mixture thickens.
3. Remove from heat and let it cool for a few minutes.
4. Divide the pudding into serving bowls and refrigerate for at least 1 hour.

Nutritional Values per Serving: Sugar: 10g; Carbohydrates: 25g; Dietary Fiber: 4g; Total Fat: 2g; Saturated Fat: 1g; Unsaturated Fat: 1g; Cholesterol: 2mg; Sodium: 30mg; Phosphorus: 100mg; Potassium: 400mg

Difficulty Rating: ☆ ☆

Tips for Ingredient Variations:
Add a sprinkle of cinnamon for extra flavor.
Top with a dollop of whipped cream or a sprinkle of chopped nuts.

112. Strawberry Yogurt Parfait

Servings: 2
Preparation time: 10 minutes
Cooking time: 0 minutes
Ingredients:
- 1 cup low-fat Greek yogurt
- 1 cup fresh strawberries, sliced
- 2 tablespoons crushed almonds
- 1 teaspoon honey (optional)

Directions:
1. In a glass or a bowl, layer Greek yogurt, sliced strawberries, and crushed almonds.
2. Repeat the layers until all the ingredients are used.
3. Drizzle with honey if desired.

Nutritional Values per Serving: Sugar: 8g; Carbohydrates: 20g; Dietary Fiber: 4g; Total Fat: 5g; Saturated Fat: 1g; Unsaturated Fat: 4g; Cholesterol: 5mg; Sodium: 20mg; Phosphorus: 150mg; Potassium: 300mg

Difficulty Rating: ☆

Tips for Ingredient Variations:
Substitute strawberries with other fresh berries like blueberries or raspberries.
Sprinkle some granola for added crunch.

113. Apple Cinnamon Mug Cake

Servings: 1
Preparation time: 5 minutes
Cooking time: 2 minutes
Ingredients:
- 1/4 cup almond flour
- 1/2 teaspoon baking powder
- 1/2 teaspoon ground cinnamon
- 1 tablespoon unsweetened applesauce
- 1 tablespoon almond milk
- 1/2 teaspoon vanilla extract
- 1 teaspoon honey (optional)

Directions:

1. In a microwave-safe mug, combine almond flour, baking powder, and ground cinnamon.

2. Add applesauce, almond milk, vanilla extract, and honey (if using). Stir until well combined.

3. Microwave on high for 1-2 minutes or until the cake is set.

4. Let it cool for a minute before enjoying.

Nutritional Values per Serving: Sugar: 4g; Carbohydrates: 10g; Dietary Fiber: 2g; Total Fat: 7g; Saturated Fat: 1g; Unsaturated Fat: 6g; Cholesterol: 0mg; Sodium: 50mg; Phosphorus: 100mg; Potassium: 150mg

Difficulty Rating: ☆☆☆

Tips for Ingredient Variations:

Add a sprinkle of nutmeg or cloves for extra warmth.

Serve with a dollop of Greek yogurt or a drizzle of sugar-free caramel sauce.

114. Chia Pudding with Berries

Servings: 2
Preparation time: 5 minutes
Cooking time: 10 minutes (inactive)
Ingredients:
- 1/4 cup chia seeds
- 1 cup unsweetened almond milk
- 1 tablespoon honey (optional)
- 1/2 cup mixed berries (strawberries, blueberries, raspberries)

Directions:

1. In a bowl, whisk together chia seeds, almond milk, and honey (if using).

2. Let the mixture sit for 10 minutes, stirring occasionally.

3. Divide the chia pudding into serving glasses or bowls.

4. Top with mixed berries and refrigerate for at least 1 hour.

Nutritional Values per Serving: Sugar: 6g; Carbohydrates: 15g; Dietary Fiber: 10g; Total Fat: 8g; Saturated Fat: 1g; Unsaturated Fat: 7g; Cholesterol: 0mg; Sodium: 50mg; Phosphorus: 200mg; Potassium: 250mg

Difficulty Rating: ☆☆

Tips for Ingredient Variations:

Add a sprinkle of cinnamon or a dash of vanilla extract for additional flavor.

Garnish with a few mint leaves for a refreshing twist.

115. Peanut Butter Energy Balls

Servings: 8
Preparation time: 10 minutes
Cooking time: 0 minutes
Ingredients:
- 1 cup old-fashioned oats
- 1/2 cup natural peanut butter
- 1/4 cup honey
- 1/4 cup unsweetened shredded coconut
- 1/4 cup mini dark chocolate chips

Directions:
1. In a mixing bowl, combine oats, peanut butter, honey, shredded coconut, and chocolate chips.
2. Mix until well combined.
3. Roll the mixture into bite-sized balls.
4. Refrigerate for at least 30 minutes before serving.

Nutritional Values per Serving: Sugar: 8g; Carbohydrates: 25g; Dietary Fiber: 4g; Total Fat: 12g; Saturated Fat: 4g; Unsaturated Fat: 8g; Cholesterol: 0mg; Sodium: 40mg; Phosphorus: 150mg; Potassium: 200mg

Difficulty Rating: ☆ ☆

Tips for Ingredient Variations:
Swap peanut butter with almond butter or cashew butter.
Add a tablespoon of flaxseed meal for an extra nutritional boost.

116. Greek Yogurt with Honey and Walnuts

Servings: 1
Preparation time: 2 minutes
Cooking time: 0 minutes
Ingredients:
- 1/2 cup low-fat Greek yogurt
- 1 tablespoon honey
- 2 tablespoons chopped walnuts

Directions:
1. In a bowl, spoon Greek yogurt.
2. Drizzle with honey and sprinkle chopped walnuts on top.
3. Mix well before enjoying.

Nutritional Values per Serving: Sugar: 12g; Carbohydrates: 20g; Dietary Fiber: 2g; Total Fat: 10g; Saturated Fat: 1g; Unsaturated Fat: 9g; Cholesterol: 5mg; Sodium: 30mg; Phosphorus: 150mg; Potassium: 200mg

Difficulty Rating: ☆

Tips for Ingredient Variations:
Replace walnuts with almonds or pecans for a different nutty flavor.
Sprinkle a pinch of cinnamon for added warmth.

117. Raspberry Chia Jam

Servings: 8
Preparation time: 5 minutes
Cooking time: 10 minutes (inactive)
Ingredients:
- 2 cups fresh raspberries
- 2 tablespoons chia seeds
- 1 tablespoon honey (optional)

Directions:
1. In a blender or food processor, puree raspberries until smooth.
2. Transfer the puree to a jar or a container.
3. Stir in chia seeds and honey (if using).
4. Refrigerate for at least 2 hours to allow the jam to thicken.

Nutritional Values per Serving: Sugar: 4g; Carbohydrates: 10g; Dietary Fiber: 6g; Total Fat: 2g; Saturated Fat: 0g; Unsaturated Fat: 2g; Cholesterol: 0mg; Sodium: 0mg; Phosphorus: 100mg; Potassium: 150mg

Difficulty Rating: ☆☆

Tips for Ingredient Variations:
Substitute raspberries with other berries like blackberries or strawberries.
Add a squeeze of lemon juice for a tangy twist.

118. Mango Coconut Chia Popsicles

Servings: 6
Preparation time: 10 minutes
Cooking time: 4 hours (inactive)
Ingredients:
- 2 ripe mangoes, peeled and pitted
- 1 cup unsweetened coconut milk
- 2 tablespoons chia seeds
- 1 tablespoon honey (optional)

Directions:
1. In a blender, puree mangoes until smooth.
2. In a bowl, whisk together coconut milk, chia seeds, and honey (if using).
3. Pour a layer of mango puree into popsicle molds, followed by a layer of coconut chia mixture.
4. Repeat the layers until the molds are filled.
5. Insert popsicle sticks and freeze for at least 4 hours or until firm.

Nutritional Values per Serving: Sugar: 10g; Carbohydrates: 20g; Dietary Fiber: 4g; Total Fat: 5g; Saturated Fat: 3g; Unsaturated Fat: 2g; Cholesterol: 0mg; Sodium: 10mg; Phosphorus: 100mg; Potassium: 250mg

Difficulty Rating: ☆☆☆

Tips for Ingredient Variations:
Add a handful of diced pineapple for an extra tropical flavor.
Sprinkle shredded coconut on top before freezing.

119. Almond Flour Blueberry Muffins

Servings: 6
Preparation time: 10 minutes
Cooking time: 12 minutes
Ingredients:
- 1 cup almond flour
- 1/4 cup coconut flour
- 1/2 teaspoon baking powder
- 1/4 teaspoon salt
- 2 tablespoons coconut oil, melted
- 2 tablespoons honey
- 2 eggs
- 1/2 cup fresh blueberries

Directions:
1. Preheat the oven to 350°F (175°C). Line a muffin tin with paper liners.
2. In a mixing bowl, combine almond flour, coconut flour, baking powder, and salt.
3. In a separate bowl, whisk together melted coconut oil, honey, and eggs.
4. Pour the wet ingredients into the dry ingredients and mix until well combined.
5. Gently fold in the blueberries.
6. Divide the batter evenly among the muffin cups.
7. Bake for 12 minutes or until a toothpick inserted into the center comes out clean.

Nutritional Values per Serving: Sugar: 6g; Carbohydrates: 15g; Dietary Fiber: 4g; Total Fat: 15g; Saturated Fat: 6g; Unsaturated Fat: 9g; Cholesterol: 60mg; Sodium: 100mg; Phosphorus: 200mg; Potassium: 200mg

Difficulty Rating: ☆☆☆

Tips for Ingredient Variations:
Replace blueberries with diced strawberries or raspberries.
Sprinkle some sliced almonds on top before baking.

120. Watermelon Fruit Pizza

Servings: 8
Preparation time: 10 minutes
Cooking time: 0 minutes
Ingredients:
- 1 small watermelon, sliced into rounds
- 1 cup low-fat Greek yogurt
- Assorted fresh fruits (strawberries, blueberries, kiwi, etc.)
- 2 tablespoons honey
- Fresh mint leaves for garnish

Directions:
1. Lay watermelon rounds on a serving platter.
2. Spread Greek yogurt evenly over the watermelon slices.
3. Arrange fresh fruits on top of the yogurt.
4. Drizzle with honey and garnish with mint leaves.

Nutritional Values per Serving: Sugar: 10g; Carbohydrates: 25g; Dietary Fiber: 4g; Total Fat: 2g; Saturated Fat: 1g; Unsaturated Fat: 1g; Cholesterol: 5mg; Sodium: 20mg; Phosphorus: 150mg; Potassium: 300mg

Difficulty Rating: ☆

Tips for Ingredient Variations:
Sprinkle some shredded coconut or granola for added texture.
Drizzle with a squeeze of lime juice for a tangy twist.

CHAPTER 18: RECIPES ON A BUDGET

121. Scrambled Eggs with Vegetables

Servings: 2
Preparation time: 5 minutes
Cooking time: 10 minutes
Ingredients:
- 4 large eggs
- 1/4 cup diced bell peppers (any color)
- 1/4 cup diced onions
- 1/4 cup diced tomatoes
- Salt and pepper to taste

Directions:
1. In a bowl, whisk the eggs until well beaten.
2. Heat a non-stick skillet over medium heat and spray with cooking spray.
3. Add the diced bell peppers, onions, and tomatoes to the skillet and sauté for 2-3 minutes until softened.
4. Pour the beaten eggs into the skillet and cook, stirring occasionally, until the eggs are cooked through.
5. Season with salt and pepper to taste.

Nutritional Values per Serving: Calories: 354 kcal; Protein: 25.8 g; Carbohydrates: 5g; Dietary Fiber: 1g; Total Fat: 10g; Saturated Fat: 3g; Cholesterol: 372mg; Sodium: 178mg; Phosphorus: 140mg; Potassium: 186mg

Difficulty Rating: ☆☆
Tips: Add mushrooms or spinach for extra flavor and nutrients.
Average cost: $2.50

122. Oatmeal with Berries and Nuts

Servings: 1
Preparation time: 5 minutes
Cooking time: 5 minutes
Ingredients:
- 1/2 cup rolled oats
- 1 cup water
- 1/4 cup mixed berries (blueberries, raspberries, strawberries)
- 1 tablespoon chopped nuts (almonds, walnuts, or pecans)
- 1 teaspoon honey (optional)

Directions:
1. In a saucepan, bring the water to a boil.
2. Add the rolled oats and reduce heat to low. Cook for 3-5 minutes, stirring occasionally, until the oats are tender, and the mixture thickens.
3. Remove from heat and transfer the oatmeal to a bowl.
4. Top with mixed berries, chopped nuts, and drizzle with honey if desired.

Nutritional Values per Serving: Calories: 265 kcal; Protein: 7.3 g; Carbohydrates: 40g; Dietary Fiber: 6g; Total Fat: 8g; Saturated Fat: 1g; Cholesterol: 0mg; Sodium: 5mg; Phosphorus: 180mg; Potassium: 240mg

Difficulty Rating: ☆
Tips: Use different types of berries or switch out the nuts for seeds like chia or flaxseeds.
Average cost: $1.50

123. Greek Yogurt Parfait

Servings: 1
Preparation time: 5 minutes
Cooking time: 0 minutes
Ingredients:

- 1/2 cup plain Greek yogurt
- 1/4 cup low-sugar granola
- 1/4 cup mixed berries (blueberries, raspberries, strawberries)
- 1 tablespoon honey (optional)

Directions:

1. In a glass or bowl, layer the Greek yogurt, granola, and mixed berries.
2. Drizzle with honey if desired.

Nutritional Values per Serving: Calories: 220 kcal; Protein: 13.5 g; Carbohydrates: 25g; Dietary Fiber: 3g; Total Fat: 4g; Saturated Fat: 0g; Cholesterol: 0mg; Sodium: 50mg; Phosphorus: 100mg; Potassium: 200mg

Difficulty Rating: ☆

Tips: Add a sprinkle of cinnamon or a tablespoon of flaxseeds for extra flavor and nutrients.

Average cost: $2.00

124. Whole Wheat Pancakes

Servings: 2
Preparation time: 10 minutes
Cooking time: 10 minutes
Ingredients:

- 1 cup whole wheat flour
- 1 tablespoon baking powder
- 1/4 teaspoon salt
- 1 tablespoon honey
- 1 cup milk (or almond milk for a dairy-free option)
- 1 large egg
- Cooking spray

Directions:

1. In a mixing bowl, whisk together the whole wheat flour, baking powder, and salt.
2. In a separate bowl, whisk together the honey, milk, and egg.
3. Pour the wet ingredients into the dry ingredients and stir until just combined.
4. Heat a non-stick skillet or griddle over medium heat and spray with cooking spray.
5. Pour 1/4 cup of batter onto the skillet for each pancake and cook until bubbles form on the surface.
6. Flip and cook for another 1-2 minutes until golden brown.

Nutritional Values per Serving: Calories: 594 kcal; Protein: 30 g; Carbohydrates: 45g; Dietary Fiber: 7g; Total Fat: 5g; Saturated Fat: 1g; Cholesterol: 93mg; Sodium: 679mg; Phosphorus: 240mg; Potassium: 320mg

Difficulty Rating: ☆ ☆

Tips: Add sliced bananas or blueberries to the pancake batter for extra flavor.

Average cost: $2.50

125. Vegetable Omelette

Servings: 1
Preparation time: 5 minutes
Cooking time: 10 minutes
Ingredients:
- 2 large eggs
- 1/4 cup diced bell peppers (any color)
- 1/4 cup diced onions
- 1/4 cup diced tomatoes
- 1/4 cup chopped spinach
- Salt and pepper to taste

Directions:
1. In a bowl, whisk the eggs until well beaten.
2. Heat a non-stick skillet over medium heat and spray with cooking spray.
3. Add the diced bell peppers, onions, tomatoes, and spinach to the skillet and sauté for 2-3 minutes until softened.
4. Pour the beaten eggs into the skillet and cook, lifting the edges to allow the uncooked eggs to flow underneath.
5. Season with salt and pepper to taste.
6. Fold the omelette in half and cook for another 1-2 minutes until the eggs are cooked through.

Nutritional Values per Serving: Calories: 202 kcal; Protein: 13.8 g; Carbohydrates: 8g; Dietary Fiber: 2g; Total Fat: 10g; Saturated Fat: 3g; Cholesterol: 372mg; Sodium: 178mg; Phosphorus: 140mg; Potassium: 186mg

Difficulty Rating: ☆☆

Tips for ingredient variations: Add mushrooms or zucchini for extra flavor and nutrients.

Average cost: $2.00

126. Avocado Toast with Egg

Servings: 1
Preparation time: 5 minutes
Cooking time: 5 minutes
Ingredients:
- 1 slice whole wheat bread
- 1/2 ripe avocado, mashed
- 1 large egg
- Salt and pepper to taste

Directions:
1. Toast the whole wheat bread.
2. Spread the mashed avocado on the toast.
3. Heat a non-stick skillet over medium heat and spray with cooking spray.
4. Crack the egg into the skillet and cook to your desired doneness.
5. Place the cooked egg on top of the avocado toast and season with salt and pepper.

Nutritional Values per Serving: Calories: 253 kcal; Protein: 11.3 g; Carbohydrates: 20g; Dietary Fiber: 8g; Total Fat: 15g; Saturated Fat: 3g; Cholesterol: 186mg; Sodium: 160mg; Phosphorus: 140mg; Potassium: 470mg

Difficulty Rating: ☆

Tips: Add sliced tomatoes or a sprinkle of feta cheese for extra flavor.

Average cost: $2.00

127. Cottage Cheese and Fruit Bowl

Servings: 1
Preparation time: 5 minutes
Cooking time: 0 minutes
Ingredients:
- 1/2 cup low-fat cottage cheese
- 1/4 cup mixed berries (blueberries, raspberries, strawberries)
- 1/4 cup diced pineapple
- 1 tablespoon chopped nuts (almonds, walnuts, or pecans)

Directions:
1. In a bowl, combine the cottage cheese, mixed berries, diced pineapple, and chopped nuts.

Nutritional Values per Serving: Calories: 209 kcal; Protein: 15.75 g; Carbohydrates: 15g; Dietary Fiber: 3g; Total Fat: 8g; Saturated Fat: 1g; Cholesterol: 10mg; Sodium: 400mg; Phosphorus: 240mg; Potassium: 220mg

Difficulty Rating: ☆

Tips: Use different fruits based on your preference or what's in season.

Average cost: $2.50

128. Breakfast Burrito

Servings: 1
Preparation time: 5 minutes
Cooking time: 10 minutes
Ingredients:
- 1 whole wheat tortilla
- 2 large eggs, scrambled
- 1/4 cup diced bell peppers (any color)
- 1/4 cup diced onions
- 1/4 cup shredded low-fat cheese
- Salsa or hot sauce (optional)

Directions:
1. Heat a non-stick skillet over medium heat and spray with cooking spray.
2. Add the diced bell peppers and onions to the skillet and sauté for 2-3 minutes until softened.
3. Add the scrambled eggs to the skillet and cook until the eggs are cooked through.
4. Warm the whole wheat tortilla in the microwave or on a skillet.
5. Place the scrambled eggs, sautéed vegetables, shredded cheese, and salsa or hot sauce (if desired) on the tortilla.
6. Fold the sides of the tortilla over the filling and roll it up.

Nutritional Values per Serving: Calories: 324 kcal; Protein: 20.4 g; Carbohydrates: 30g; Dietary Fiber: 5g; Total Fat: 15g; Saturated Fat: 5g; Cholesterol: 372mg; Sodium: 400mg; Phosphorus: 220mg; Potassium: 260mg

Difficulty Rating: ☆ ☆

Tips: Add diced tomatoes, avocado slices, or black beans for extra flavor and nutrients.

Average cost: $3.00

129. Fruit and Yogurt Smoothie

Servings: 1
Preparation time: 5 minutes
Cooking time: 0 minutes
Ingredients:
- 1/2 cup plain Greek yogurt
- 1/2 cup mixed berries (blueberries, raspberries, strawberries)
- 1/2 banana
- 1/2 cup unsweetened almond milk (or any milk of your choice)
- 1 tablespoon honey (optional)

Directions:
1. In a blender, combine the Greek yogurt, mixed berries, banana, almond milk, and honey (if desired).
2. Blend until smooth and creamy.

Nutritional Values per Serving: Calories: 187 kcal; Protein: 11.6 g; Carbohydrates: 30g; Dietary Fiber: 5g; Total Fat: 2g; Saturated Fat: 0g; Cholesterol: 0mg; Sodium: 100mg; Phosphorus: 160mg; Potassium: 470mg

Difficulty Rating: ☆
Tips: Add a handful of spinach or kale for an extra boost of nutrients.
Average cost: $2.50

130. Veggie Breakfast Wrap

Servings: 1
Preparation time: 10 minutes
Cooking time: 5 minutes
Ingredients:
- 1 whole wheat tortilla
- 2 large eggs, scrambled
- 1/4 cup diced bell peppers (any color)
- 1/4 cup diced onions
- 1/4 cup diced tomatoes
- 1/4 cup chopped spinach
- Salt and pepper to taste

Directions:
1. Heat a non-stick skillet over medium heat and spray with cooking spray.
2. Add the diced bell peppers, onions, tomatoes, and spinach to the skillet and sauté for 2-3 minutes until softened.
3. Add the scrambled eggs to the skillet and cook until the eggs are cooked through.
4. Warm the whole wheat tortilla in the microwave or on a skillet.
5. Place the scrambled eggs and sautéed vegetables on the tortilla.
6. Season with salt and pepper to taste.
7. Fold the sides of the tortilla over the filling and roll it up.

Nutritional Values per Serving: Calories: 296 kcal; Protein: 13.8 g; Carbohydrates: 35g; Dietary Fiber: 7g; Total Fat: 10g; Saturated Fat: 3g; Cholesterol: 372mg; Sodium: 260mg; Phosphorus: 180mg; Potassium: 320mg

Difficulty Rating: ☆ ☆
Tips: Add sliced avocado or a dollop of Greek yogurt for extra creaminess.
Average cost: $2.50

131. Chicken and Vegetable Stir-Fry

Servings: 2
Preparation time: 10 minutes
Cooking time: 15 minutes
Ingredients:
- 1 boneless, skinless chicken breast, sliced
- 1 cup mixed vegetables (broccoli, bell peppers, carrots)
- 2 cloves garlic, minced
- 1 tablespoon low-sodium soy sauce
- 1 teaspoon sesame oil
- 1/2 teaspoon ginger, grated
- Salt and pepper to taste

Directions:
1. Heat sesame oil in a pan over medium heat.
2. Add minced garlic and grated ginger, sauté for a minute.
3. Add sliced chicken breast and cook until no longer pink.
4. Add mixed vegetables and cook until tender-crisp.
5. Stir in low-sodium soy sauce, salt, and pepper.
6. Serve hot with a side of brown rice or quinoa.

Nutritional Values per Serving: Calories: 405 kcal; Protein: 49.8 g; Carbohydrates: 15g; Dietary Fiber: 4g; Total Fat: 5g; Saturated Fat: 1g; Cholesterol: 45mg; Sodium: 300mg; Phosphorus: 200mg; Potassium: 400mg

Difficulty Rating: ☆☆

Tips: You can add other vegetables like snap peas or mushrooms for more variety. For a renal diet variation, reduce the amount of soy sauce or use a low-sodium alternative.

132. Turkey and Avocado Wrap

Servings: 1
Preparation time: 5 minutes
Cooking time: N/A
Ingredients:
- 2 slices of low-sodium turkey breast
- 1/4 avocado, sliced
- 1 whole wheat tortilla
- 1 tablespoon Greek yogurt
- 1/2 cup mixed greens
- Salt and pepper to taste

Directions:
1. Lay the whole wheat tortilla flat on a clean surface.
2. Spread Greek yogurt evenly on the tortilla.
3. Layer turkey slices, avocado slices, and mixed greens on top.
4. Season with salt and pepper.
5. Roll the tortilla tightly, tucking in the sides as you go.
6. Slice in half and serve.

Nutritional Values per Serving: Calories: 351 kcal; Protein: 24.4 g; Carbohydrates: 30g; Dietary Fiber: 8g; Total Fat: 10g; Saturated Fat: 2g; Cholesterol: 25mg; Sodium: 200mg; Phosphorus: 150mg; Potassium: 350mg

Difficulty Rating: ☆

Tips: You can add other vegetables like sliced cucumbers or tomatoes for extra crunch and flavor. For a renal diet variation, use low-sodium turkey breast slices and limit the amount of added salt.

133. Tuna Salad Lettuce Wraps

Servings: 2
Preparation time: 10 minutes
Cooking time: N/A
Ingredients:
- 1 can of tuna in water, drained
- 2 tablespoons mayonnaise (low-fat or light)
- 1 tablespoon Dijon mustard
- 1 celery stalk, diced
- 1/4 red onion, diced
- Salt and pepper to taste
- 4 large lettuce leaves

Directions:
1. In a bowl, combine tuna, mayonnaise, Dijon mustard, diced celery, and red onion.
2. Mix well until all ingredients are evenly incorporated.
3. Season with salt and pepper.
4. Spoon the tuna salad onto the lettuce leaves.
5. Wrap the lettuce leaves around the filling, securing with toothpicks if necessary.
6. Serve chilled.

Nutritional Values per Serving: Calories: 211 kcal; Protein: 22.8 g; Carbohydrates: 5g; Dietary Fiber: 2g; Total Fat: 8g; Saturated Fat: 1g; Cholesterol: 20mg; Sodium: 300mg; Phosphorus: 150mg; Potassium: 250mg

Difficulty Rating: ☆☆

Tips: You can add diced pickles or cherry tomatoes to the tuna salad for added flavor and texture. For a renal diet variation, use low-sodium tuna and limit the amount of added salt.

134. Lentil and Vegetable Soup

Servings: 4
Preparation time: 10 minutes
Cooking time: 30 minutes
Ingredients:
- 1 cup dried lentils, rinsed and drained
- 1 onion, diced
- 2 carrots, diced
- 2 celery stalks, diced
- 2 cloves garlic, minced
- 4 cups low-sodium vegetable broth
- 1 teaspoon cumin
- 1/2 teaspoon paprika
- Salt and pepper to taste

Directions:
1. In a large pot, sauté onion, carrots, celery, and garlic until softened.
2. Add lentils, vegetable broth, cumin, and paprika.
3. Bring to a boil, then reduce heat and simmer for 25-30 minutes until lentils are tender.
4. Season with salt and pepper.
5. Serve hot.

Nutritional Values per Serving: Calories: 363 kcal; Protein: 19 g; Carbohydrates: 30g; Dietary Fiber: 12g; Total Fat: 1g; Saturated Fat: 0g; Cholesterol: 0mg; Sodium: 200mg; Phosphorus: 250mg; Potassium: 600mg

Difficulty Rating: ☆☆

Tips: You can add other vegetables like zucchini or spinach for added nutrition. For a renal diet variation, limit the amount of added salt and use low-sodium vegetable broth.

135. Quinoa and Vegetable Salad

Servings: 2
Preparation time: 15 minutes
Cooking time: 15 minutes
Ingredients:
- 1/2 cup quinoa, rinsed
- 1 cup water
- 1/2 cucumber, diced
- 1/2 bell pepper, diced
- 1/4 red onion, diced
- 1/4 cup cherry tomatoes, halved
- 2 tablespoons lemon juice
- 1 tablespoon olive oil
- Salt and pepper to taste

Directions:
1. In a saucepan, bring water to a boil.
2. Add quinoa, reduce heat, cover, and simmer for 15 minutes until water is absorbed and quinoa is tender.
3. In a bowl, combine cooked quinoa, cucumber, bell pepper, red onion, and cherry tomatoes.
4. In a separate small bowl, whisk together lemon juice, olive oil, salt, and pepper.
5. Pour the dressing over the quinoa and vegetable mixture, tossing to coat evenly.
6. Serve chilled or at room temperature.

Nutritional Values per Serving: Calories: 425 kcal; Protein: 10.1 g; Carbohydrates: 35g; Dietary Fiber: 6g; Total Fat: 6g; Saturated Fat: 1g; Cholesterol: 0mg; Sodium: 100mg; Phosphorus: 200mg; Potassium: 400mg

Difficulty Rating: ☆

Tips: You can add chopped fresh herbs like parsley or basil for extra flavor. For a renal diet variation, use low-sodium vegetable broth to cook the quinoa and limit the amount of added salt.

136. Spinach and Mushroom Omelette

Servings: 1
Preparation time: 5 minutes
Cooking time: 10 minutes
Ingredients:
- 2 eggs
- 1 cup fresh spinach leaves
- 4-5 button mushrooms, sliced
- 1/4 onion, diced
- 1 tablespoon olive oil
- Salt and pepper to taste

Directions:
1. In a bowl, whisk the eggs until well beaten.
2. Heat olive oil in a non-stick skillet over medium heat.
3. Add diced onion and sliced mushrooms, sauté until softened.
4. Add fresh spinach leaves and cook until wilted.
5. Pour the beaten eggs over the vegetables, spreading them evenly.
6. Cook until the omelette is set, then flip and cook for another minute.
7. Season with salt and pepper.
8. Serve hot.

Nutritional Values per Serving: Calories: 306 kcal; Protein: 15 g; Carbohydrates: 8g; Dietary Fiber: 2g; Total Fat: 15g; Saturated Fat: 3g; Cholesterol: 370mg; Sodium: 200mg; Phosphorus: 250mg; Potassium: 400mg

Difficulty Rating: ☆ ☆

Tips: You can add low-fat cheese or diced tomatoes for added flavor. For a renal diet variation, limit the amount of added salt and use a non-stick skillet to reduce the need for oil.

137. Black Bean and Vegetable Quesadilla

Servings: 2
Preparation time: 10 minutes
Cooking time: 10 minutes
Ingredients:
- 4 small whole wheat tortillas
- 1/2 cup black beans, rinsed and drained
- 1/4 cup corn kernels
- 1/4 cup diced bell peppers
- 1/4 cup shredded low-fat cheese
- 1/4 teaspoon cumin
- 1/4 teaspoon chili powder
- Salt and pepper to taste

Directions:
1. Lay two tortillas flat on a clean surface.
2. Divide black beans, corn kernels, diced bell peppers, and shredded cheese evenly between the two tortillas.
3. Sprinkle with cumin, chili powder, salt, and pepper.
4. Top with the remaining two tortillas.
5. Heat a non-stick skillet over medium heat.
6. Cook each quesadilla for 2-3 minutes on each side until cheese is melted, and tortillas are crispy.
7. Slice into wedges and serve hot.

Nutritional Values per Serving:
Calories: 650 kcal; Protein: 23.7 g; Carbohydrates: 35g; Dietary Fiber: 8g; Total Fat: 6g; Saturated Fat: 2g; Cholesterol: 10mg; Sodium: 300mg; Phosphorus: 200mg; Potassium: 400mg

Difficulty Rating: ☆

Tips: You can add sliced avocado or diced tomatoes as a topping. For a renal diet variation, use low-sodium black beans and limit the amount of added salt.

138. Greek Salad with Grilled Chicken

Servings: 2
Preparation time: 15 minutes
Cooking time: 15 minutes
Ingredients:
- 2 boneless, skinless chicken breasts
- 2 cups mixed salad greens
- 1/2 cucumber, diced
- 1/2 bell pepper, diced
- 1/4 red onion, thinly sliced
- 1/4 cup Kalamata olives
- 1/4 cup crumbled feta cheese
- 2 tablespoons lemon juice
- 1 tablespoon olive oil
- Salt and pepper to taste

Directions:
1. Preheat a grill or grill pan over medium-high heat.
2. Season chicken breasts with salt and pepper.
3. Grill chicken for 6-8 minutes per side until cooked through.
4. Let the chicken rest for a few minutes, then slice into thin strips.
5. In a large bowl, combine mixed salad greens, diced cucumber, diced bell pepper, thinly sliced red onion, Kalamata olives, and crumbled feta cheese.
6. In a separate small bowl, whisk together lemon juice, olive oil, salt, and pepper.
7. Pour the dressing over the salad mixture, tossing to coat evenly.
8. Top the salad with grilled chicken slices.
9. Serve chilled.

Nutritional Values per Serving:
Calories: 584 kcal; Protein: 67.6 g; Carbohydrates: 10g; Dietary Fiber: 3g; Total Fat: 15g; Saturated Fat: 5g; Cholesterol: 80mg; Sodium: 400mg; Phosphorus: 250mg; Potassium: 600mg

Difficulty Rating: ☆ ☆

Tips: You can add cherry tomatoes or sliced avocado for extra flavor. For a renal diet variation, use low-sodium feta cheese and limit the amount of added salt.

139. Salmon and Asparagus Foil Packets

Servings: 2
Preparation time: 10 minutes
Cooking time: 20 minutes
Ingredients:
- 2 salmon fillets
- 1 bunch asparagus, trimmed
- 1 lemon, sliced
- 2 cloves garlic, minced
- 1 tablespoon olive oil
- Salt and pepper to taste

Directions:
1. Preheat the oven to 400°F (200°C).
2. Cut two large pieces of aluminum foil.
3. Place a salmon fillet on each piece of foil.
4. Arrange asparagus spears and lemon slices around the salmon.
5. Drizzle with olive oil and sprinkle minced garlic, salt, and pepper.
6. Fold the foil over the salmon and vegetables, sealing the edges tightly.
7. Place the foil packets on a baking sheet and bake for 15-20 minutes until salmon is cooked through.
8. Serve hot.

Nutritional Values per Serving: Calories: 601 kcal; Protein: 46.4 g; Carbohydrates: 10g; Dietary Fiber: 4g; Total Fat: 15g; Saturated Fat: 2g; Cholesterol: 70mg; Sodium: 200mg; Phosphorus: 350mg; Potassium: 800mg

Difficulty Rating: ☆☆

Tips: You can add sliced cherry tomatoes or sprinkle fresh dill on top before baking. For a renal diet variation, limit the amount of added salt.

140. Veggie and Hummus Wrap

Servings: 1
Preparation time: 5 minutes
Cooking time: N/A
Ingredients:
- 1 whole wheat tortilla
- 2 tablespoons hummus
- 1/4 cucumber, sliced
- 1/4 bell pepper, sliced
- 1/4 carrot, julienned
- 1/4 cup mixed salad greens
- Salt and pepper to taste

Directions:
1. Lay the whole wheat tortilla flat on a clean surface.
2. Spread hummus evenly on the tortilla.
3. Layer cucumber slices, bell pepper slices, julienned carrot, and mixed salad greens on top.
4. Season with salt and pepper.
5. Roll the tortilla tightly, tucking in the sides as you go.
6. Slice in half and serve.

Nutritional Values per Serving: Calories: 241 kcal; Protein: 9.6 g; Carbohydrates: 35g; Dietary Fiber: 8g; Total Fat: 6g; Saturated Fat: 1g; Cholesterol: 0mg; Sodium: 300mg; Phosphorus: 150mg; Potassium: 400mg

Difficulty Rating: ☆

Tips: You can add sliced avocado or sprinkle with lemon juice for extra flavor. For a renal diet variation, use low-sodium hummus and limit the amount of added salt.

141. Grilled Lemon Herb Chicken Breast

Servings: 4
Preparation time: 10 minutes
Cooking time: 15 minutes
Ingredients:
- 4 boneless, skinless chicken breasts
- 2 tablespoons olive oil
- 1 tablespoon lemon juice
- 1 teaspoon dried thyme
- 1 teaspoon dried rosemary
- Salt and pepper to taste

Directions:
1. Preheat the grill to medium-high heat.
2. In a small bowl, mix together the olive oil, lemon juice, thyme, rosemary, salt, and pepper.
3. Brush the chicken breasts with the herb mixture.
4. Grill the chicken for about 6-8 minutes per side, or until cooked through.
5. Serve hot with a side of steamed vegetables.

Nutritional Values per Serving: Calories: 828 kcal; Protein: 124 g; Carbohydrates: 0g; Dietary Fiber: 0g; Total Fat: 9g; Saturated Fat: 2g; Cholesterol: 86mg; Sodium: 67mg; Phosphorus: 215mg; Potassium: 296mg

Difficulty Rating: ☆ ☆

Tips: For a renal diet variation, reduce the amount of salt used in the marinade.

142. Baked Salmon with Dill Sauce

Servings: 2
Preparation time: 5 minutes
Cooking time: 15 minutes
Ingredients:
- 2 salmon fillets
- 2 tablespoons lemon juice
- 1 tablespoon fresh dill, chopped
- 1 clove garlic, minced
- Salt and pepper to taste

Directions:
1. Preheat the oven to 400°F (200°C).
2. Place the salmon fillets on a baking sheet lined with parchment paper.
3. In a small bowl, mix together the lemon juice, dill, garlic, salt, and pepper.
4. Brush the dill sauce over the salmon fillets.
5. Bake for 12-15 minutes, or until the salmon is cooked through and flakes easily with a fork.
6. Serve hot with a side of roasted asparagus.

Nutritional Values per Serving: Calories: 504 kcal; Protein: 44 g; Carbohydrates: 1g; Dietary Fiber: 0g; Total Fat: 21g; Saturated Fat: 5g; Cholesterol: 62mg; Sodium: 73mg; Phosphorus: 249mg; Potassium: 534mg

Difficulty Rating: ☆ ☆ ☆

Tips: For a renal diet variation, use low-sodium soy sauce instead of salt in the dill sauce.

143. Turkey and Vegetable Stir-Fry

Servings: 4
Preparation time: 15 minutes
Cooking time: 15 minutes
Ingredients:
- 1 pound turkey breast, cut into thin strips
- 2 tablespoons low-sodium soy sauce
- 1 tablespoon sesame oil
- 1 teaspoon ginger, grated
- 2 cloves garlic, minced
- 2 cups mixed vegetables (broccoli, bell peppers, carrots, snap peas)
- Salt and pepper to taste

Directions:
1. In a bowl, combine the turkey strips, soy sauce, sesame oil, ginger, and garlic. Let it marinate for 10 minutes.
2. Heat a large skillet or wok over medium-high heat. Add the marinated turkey and cook until browned.
3. Add the mixed vegetables to the skillet and stir-fry for 5-7 minutes, or until crisp-tender.
4. Season with salt and pepper to taste.
5. Serve hot with a side of brown rice.

Nutritional Values per Serving: Calories: 360 kcal; Protein: 35 g; Carbohydrates: 8g; Dietary Fiber: 2g; Total Fat: 4g; Saturated Fat: 1g; Cholesterol: 62mg; Sodium: 304mg; Phosphorus: 255mg; Potassium: 528mg

Difficulty Rating: ☆☆☆

Tips: For a renal diet variation, use low-sodium soy sauce, and limit the amount of salt added.

144. Quinoa and Black Bean Salad

Servings: 6
Preparation time: 15 minutes
Cooking time: 20 minutes
Ingredients:
- 1 cup quinoa, rinsed
- 2 cups water
- 1 can (15 ounces) black beans, rinsed and drained
- 1 cup cherry tomatoes, halved
- 1/2 cup red onion, finely chopped
- 1/4 cup fresh cilantro, chopped
- 2 tablespoons lime juice
- 2 tablespoons olive oil
- Salt and pepper to taste

Directions:
1. In a medium saucepan, bring the water to a boil. Add the quinoa and reduce heat to low. Cover and simmer for 15-20 minutes, or until the quinoa is tender and the water is absorbed.
2. In a large bowl, combine the cooked quinoa, black beans, cherry tomatoes, red onion, and cilantro.
3. In a small bowl, whisk together the lime juice, olive oil, salt, and pepper. Pour the dressing over the quinoa mixture and toss to combine.
4. Serve chilled as a refreshing salad.

Nutritional Values per Serving: Calories: 1864 kcal; Protein: 31 g; Carbohydrates: 30g; Dietary Fiber: 7g; Total Fat: 6g; Saturated Fat: 1g; Cholesterol: 0mg; Sodium: 196mg; Phosphorus: 218mg; Potassium: 491mg

Difficulty Rating: ☆☆

Tips: For a renal diet variation, rinse the canned black beans thoroughly to remove excess sodium.

145. Vegetable Curry with Brown Rice

Servings: 4
Preparation time: 10 minutes
Cooking time: 25 minutes
Ingredients:
- 1 tablespoon olive oil
- 1 onion, chopped
- 2 cloves garlic, minced
- 1 tablespoon curry powder
- 1 teaspoon ground cumin
- 1/2 teaspoon ground turmeric
- 1 can (14 ounces) diced tomatoes
- 1 can (14 ounces) coconut milk
- 2 cups mixed vegetables (cauliflower, carrots, peas, bell peppers)
- Salt and pepper to taste
- 2 cups cooked brown rice

Directions:
1. Heat the olive oil in a large skillet over medium heat. Add the onion and garlic and cook until softened.
2. Stir in the curry powder, cumin, and turmeric. Cook for an additional minute.
3. Add the diced tomatoes (with their juice) and coconut milk to the skillet. Bring to a simmer.
4. Add the mixed vegetables and season with salt and pepper. Cook for 10-15 minutes, or until the vegetables are tender.
5. Serve the vegetable curry over cooked brown rice.

Nutritional Values per Serving: Calories: 514 kcal; Protein: 13 g; Carbohydrates: 50g; Dietary Fiber: 8g; Total Fat: 19g; Saturated Fat: 14g; Cholesterol: 0mg; Sodium: 259mg; Phosphorus: 241mg; Potassium: 780mg

Difficulty Rating: ☆ ☆ ☆

Tips: For a renal diet variation, use low-sodium diced tomatoes and limit the amount of salt added.

146. Spinach and Feta Stuffed Chicken Breast

Servings: 2
Preparation time: 15 minutes
Cooking time: 25 minutes
Ingredients:
- 2 boneless, skinless chicken breasts
- 2 cups fresh spinach, chopped
- 1/4 cup crumbled feta cheese
- 1 clove garlic, minced
- Salt and pepper to taste

Directions:
1. Preheat the oven to 375°F (190°C).
2. Cut a slit lengthwise through each chicken breast to create a pocket.
3. In a bowl, combine the chopped spinach, feta cheese, garlic, salt, and pepper.
4. Stuff each chicken breast with the spinach and feta mixture, pressing the edges to seal.
5. Place the stuffed chicken breasts on a baking sheet lined with parchment paper.
6. Bake for 20-25 minutes, or until the chicken is cooked through.
7. Serve hot with a side of roasted sweet potatoes.

Nutritional Values per Serving: Calories: 444 kcal; Protein: 66.9 g; Carbohydrates: 2g; Dietary Fiber: 1g; Total Fat: 9g; Saturated Fat: 4g; Cholesterol: 86mg; Sodium: 214mg; Phosphorus: 245mg; Potassium: 441mg

Difficulty Rating: ☆ ☆ ☆

Tips: For a renal diet variation, use low-sodium feta cheese and limit the amount of salt added.

147. Lentil and Vegetable Soup

Servings: 6
Preparation time: 10 minutes
Cooking time: 30 minutes
Ingredients:
- 1 tablespoon olive oil
- 1 onion, chopped
- 2 carrots, diced
- 2 stalks celery, diced
- 2 cloves garlic, minced
- 1 cup dried lentils
- 4 cups low-sodium vegetable broth
- 1 can (14 ounces) diced tomatoes
- 2 cups chopped kale
- Salt and pepper to taste

Directions:
1. Heat the olive oil in a large pot over medium heat. Add the onion, carrots, celery, and garlic. Cook until the vegetables are softened.
2. Add the dried lentils, vegetable broth, and diced tomatoes to the pot. Bring to a boil, then reduce heat to low and simmer for 20-25 minutes, or until the lentils are tender.
3. Stir in the chopped kale and cook for an additional 5 minutes, or until wilted.
4. Season with salt and pepper to taste.
5. Serve hot as a comforting soup.

Nutritional Values per Serving: Calories: 1963 kcal; Protein: 24 g; Carbohydrates: 30g; Dietary Fiber: 12g; Total Fat: 3g; Saturated Fat: 0g; Cholesterol: 0mg; Sodium: 197mg; Phosphorus: 232mg; Potassium: 847mg

Difficulty Rating: ☆ ☆

Tips: For a renal diet variation, use low-sodium vegetable broth and limit the amount of salt added.

148. Shrimp and Broccoli Stir-Fry

Servings: 2
Preparation time: 10 minutes
Cooking time: 10 minutes
Ingredients:
- 1 tablespoon olive oil
- 1/2 pound shrimp, peeled and deveined
- 2 cups broccoli florets
- 1 bell pepper, sliced
- 2 cloves garlic, minced
- 2 tablespoons low-sodium soy sauce
- 1 tablespoon rice vinegar
- 1/2 teaspoon ginger, grated
- Salt and pepper to taste

Directions:
1. Heat the olive oil in a large skillet or wok over medium-high heat. Add the shrimp and cook until pink and cooked through. Remove from the skillet and set aside.
2. In the same skillet, add the broccoli florets, bell pepper, and garlic. Stir-fry for 5-7 minutes, or until the vegetables are crisp-tender.
3. In a small bowl, whisk together the soy sauce, rice vinegar, ginger, salt, and pepper. Pour the sauce over the vegetables and stir to coat.
4. Add the cooked shrimp back to the skillet and cook for an additional 2 minutes, or until heated through.
5. Serve hot with a side of brown rice.

Nutritional Values per Serving: Calories: 287 kcal; Protein: 26.6 g; Carbohydrates: 11g; Dietary Fiber: 4g; Total Fat: 8g; Saturated Fat: 1g; Cholesterol: 143mg; Sodium: 501mg; Phosphorus: 217mg; Potassium: 527mg

Difficulty Rating: ☆ ☆

Tips: For a renal diet variation, use low-sodium soy sauce and limit the amount of salt added.

149. Eggplant Parmesan

Servings: 4
Preparation time: 15 minutes
Cooking time: 30 minutes
Ingredients:

- 1 large eggplant, sliced into rounds
- 1 cup whole wheat breadcrumbs
- 1/2 cup grated Parmesan cheese
- 2 eggs, beaten
- 2 cups marinara sauce
- 1 cup shredded mozzarella cheese
- Salt and pepper to taste

Directions:

1. Preheat the oven to 375°F (190°C).
2. Season the eggplant slices with salt and pepper. Let them sit for 10 minutes to remove excess moisture, then pat dry with a paper towel.
3. In a shallow dish, combine the breadcrumbs and Parmesan cheese.
4. Dip each eggplant slice into the beaten eggs, then coat with the breadcrumb mixture.
5. Place the coated eggplant slices on a baking sheet lined with parchment paper.
6. Bake for 15 minutes, or until the eggplant is tender, and the breadcrumbs are golden.
7. Spread a thin layer of marinara sauce on the bottom of a baking dish. Arrange half of the baked eggplant slices on top.
8. Top with another layer of marinara sauce and sprinkle with half of the shredded mozzarella cheese.
9. Repeat the layers with the remaining eggplant slices, marinara sauce, and mozzarella cheese.
10. Bake for 15 minutes, or until the cheese is melted and bubbly.
11. Serve hot as a delicious vegetarian dinner.

Nutritional Values per Serving: Calories: 1135 kcal; Protein: 51.2 g; Carbohydrates: 32g; Dietary Fiber: 8g; Total Fat: 15g; Saturated Fat: 7g; Cholesterol: 112mg; Sodium: 898mg; Phosphorus: 312mg; Potassium: 614mg

Difficulty Rating: ☆☆☆

Tips: For a renal diet variation, use low-sodium marinara sauce and limit the amount of salt added.

150. Greek Salad with Grilled Chicken

Servings: 2
Preparation time: 15 minutes
Cooking time: 15 minutes
Ingredients:

- 2 boneless, skinless chicken breasts
- 2 tablespoons lemon juice
- 2 tablespoons olive oil
- 1 teaspoon dried oregano
- Salt and pepper to taste
- 2 cups mixed salad greens
- 1/2 cup cherry tomatoes, halved
- 1/4 cup cucumber, diced
- 1/4 cup red onion, thinly sliced
- 1/4 cup Kalamata olives
- 1/4 cup crumbled feta cheese
- 2 tablespoons Greek dressing

Directions:

1. Preheat the grill to medium-high heat.
2. In a small bowl, whisk together the lemon juice, olive oil, dried oregano, salt, and pepper.
3. Brush the chicken breasts with the marinade.
4. Grill the chicken for about 6-8 minutes per side, or until cooked through.
5. Let the chicken rest for a few minutes, then slice into strips.
6. In a large bowl, combine the mixed salad greens, cherry tomatoes, cucumber, red onion, Kalamata olives, and crumbled feta cheese.
7. Drizzle with the Greek dressing and toss to coat.
8. Top the salad with the grilled chicken slices.
9. Serve chilled as a refreshing and protein-packed dinner.

Nutritional Values per Serving: Calories: 666 kcal; Protein: 66 g; Carbohydrates: 9g; Dietary Fiber: 2g; Total Fat: 21g; Saturated Fat: 6g; Cholesterol: 86mg; Sodium: 454mg; Phosphorus: 266mg; Potassium: 518mg

Difficulty Rating: ☆☆

Tips: For a renal diet variation, use low-sodium Greek dressing and limit the amount of salt added.

151. Roasted Chickpeas

Servings: 4
Preparation time: 5 minutes
Cooking time: 25 minutes
Ingredients:

- 2 cans of chickpeas, drained and rinsed
- 1 tablespoon olive oil
- 1 teaspoon paprika
- 1/2 teaspoon garlic powder
- 1/2 teaspoon cumin
- Salt to taste

Directions:

1. Preheat the oven to 400°F (200°C).
2. In a bowl, toss the chickpeas with olive oil, paprika, garlic powder, cumin, and salt.
3. Spread the chickpeas in a single layer on a baking sheet.
4. Roast in the oven for 20-25 minutes, or until crispy, stirring once halfway through.

Nutritional Values per Serving: Calories: 238 kcal; Protein: 116 g; Carbohydrates: 22g; Dietary Fiber: 5g; Total Fat: 5g; Saturated Fat: 1g; Cholesterol: 0mg; Sodium: 150mg; Phosphorus: 70mg; Potassium: 250mg

Difficulty Rating: ☆☆

Tips: Add a pinch of cayenne pepper for a spicy kick.

152. Greek Yogurt Parfait

Servings: 1
Preparation time: 5 minutes
Ingredients:

- 1/2 cup plain Greek yogurt
- 1/4 cup fresh berries (such as strawberries, blueberries, or raspberries)
- 1 tablespoon chopped nuts (such as almonds or walnuts)
- 1 teaspoon honey (optional)

Directions:

1. In a glass or bowl, layer the Greek yogurt, fresh berries, and chopped nuts.
2. Drizzle with honey, if desired.

Nutritional Values per Serving: Calories: 109 kcal; Protein: 11.75 g; Carbohydrates: 15g; Dietary Fiber: 2g; Total Fat: 6g; Saturated Fat: 1g; Cholesterol: 5mg; Sodium: 25mg; Phosphorus: 150mg; Potassium: 200mg

Difficulty Rating: ☆

Tips: Use frozen berries if fresh ones are not available.

153. Veggie Sticks with Hummus

Servings: 2
Preparation time: 10 minutes
Ingredients:
- 2 medium carrots, cut into sticks
- 2 medium cucumbers, cut into sticks
- 1/2 cup hummus

Directions:
1. Arrange the carrot and cucumber sticks on a plate.
2. Serve with hummus for dipping.

Nutritional Values per Serving: Calories: 207 kcal; Protein: 7.4 g; Carbohydrates: 15g; Dietary Fiber: 6g; Total Fat: 10g; Saturated Fat: 1g; Cholesterol: 0mg; Sodium: 200mg; Phosphorus: 100mg; Potassium: 400mg

Difficulty Rating: ☆

Tips: Try using different vegetables like bell peppers or celery.

154. Baked Sweet Potato Chips

Servings: 2
Preparation time: 10 minutes
Cooking time: 25 minutes
Ingredients:
- 2 medium sweet potatoes, thinly sliced
- 1 tablespoon olive oil
- 1/2 teaspoon paprika
- 1/4 teaspoon garlic powder
- Salt to taste

Directions:
1. Preheat the oven to 400°F (200°C).
2. In a bowl, toss the sweet potato slices with olive oil, paprika, garlic powder, and salt.
3. Arrange the slices in a single layer on a baking sheet.
4. Bake for 20-25 minutes, or until crispy, flipping once halfway through.

Nutritional Values per Serving: Calories: 576 kcal; Protein: 8 g; Carbohydrates: 20g; Dietary Fiber: 3g; Total Fat: 5g; Saturated Fat: 1g; Cholesterol: 0mg; Sodium: 100mg; Phosphorus: 80mg; Potassium: 400mg

Difficulty Rating: ☆ ☆

Tips: Sprinkle with a pinch of cinnamon for a sweet twist.

155. Tuna Salad Lettuce Wraps

Servings: 2
Preparation time: 10 minutes
Ingredients:
- 1 can tuna, drained
- 2 tablespoons mayonnaise
- 1 tablespoon diced celery
- 1 tablespoon diced red onion
- Salt and pepper to taste
- 4 large lettuce leaves

Directions:
1. In a bowl, mix together the tuna, mayonnaise, celery, red onion, salt, and pepper.
2. Spoon the tuna salad onto the lettuce leaves.
3. Roll up the lettuce leaves to form wraps.

Nutritional Values per Serving: Calories: 446 kcal; Protein: 44.4 g; Carbohydrates: 4g; Dietary Fiber: 1g; Total Fat: 10g; Saturated Fat: 2g; Cholesterol: 25mg; Sodium: 300mg; Phosphorus: 150mg; Potassium: 200mg

Difficulty Rating: ☆ ☆

Tips: Add chopped pickles or olives for extra flavor.

156. Apple Slices with Peanut Butter

Servings: 2
Preparation time: 5 minutes
Ingredients:
- 1 medium apple, sliced
- 2 tablespoons peanut butter

Directions:
1. Arrange the apple slices on a plate.
2. Serve with peanut butter for dipping.

Nutritional Values per Serving: Calories: 387 kcal; Protein: 9 g; Carbohydrates: 20g; Dietary Fiber: 4g; Total Fat: 10g; Saturated Fat: 2g; Cholesterol: 0mg; Sodium: 100mg; Phosphorus: 100mg; Potassium: 200mg

Difficulty Rating: ☆

Tips: Use almond butter or sunflower seed butter as an alternative.

157. Cottage Cheese and Berries

Servings: 1
Preparation time: 5 minutes
Ingredients:
- 1/2 cup low-fat cottage cheese
- 1/4 cup fresh berries (such as strawberries, blueberries, or raspberries)
- **Directions:**

1. In a bowl, combine the cottage cheese and fresh berries.

Nutritional Values per Serving: Calories: 116 kcal; Protein: 14.5 g; Carbohydrates: 10g; Dietary Fiber: 2g; Total Fat: 2g; Saturated Fat: 1g; Cholesterol: 10mg; Sodium: 200mg; Phosphorus: 150mg; Potassium: 200mg

Difficulty Rating: ☆

Tips: Sprinkle with a dash of cinnamon for added flavor.

158. Mini Caprese Skewers

Servings: 4
Preparation time: 10 minutes
Ingredients:
- 8 cherry tomatoes
- 8 small mozzarella balls
- 8 small basil leaves
- 1 tablespoon balsamic glaze

Directions:

1. Thread a cherry tomato, mozzarella ball, and basil leaf onto a skewer.
2. Repeat with the remaining ingredients.
3. Drizzle with balsamic glaze before serving.

Nutritional Values per Serving: Calories: 236 kcal; Protein: 40 g; Carbohydrates: 4g; Dietary Fiber: 1g; Total Fat: 6g; Saturated Fat: 3g; Cholesterol: 15mg; Sodium: 100mg; Phosphorus: 100mg; Potassium: 100mg

Difficulty Rating: ☆

Tips: Use toothpicks if skewers are not available.

159. Hard-Boiled Eggs with Salt and Pepper

Servings: 2
Preparation time: 5 minutes
Cooking time: 10 minutes
Ingredients:

- 2 large eggs
- Salt and pepper to taste

Directions:

1. Place the eggs in a saucepan and cover with water.
2. Bring the water to a boil, then reduce the heat and simmer for 8-10 minutes.
3. Remove the eggs from the water and let them cool slightly.
4. Peel the eggs and sprinkle with salt and pepper.

Nutritional Values per Serving: Calories: 304 kcal; Protein: 24 g; Carbohydrates: 1g; Dietary Fiber: 0g; Total Fat: 5g; Saturated Fat: 2g; Cholesterol: 185mg; Sodium: 70mg; Phosphorus: 100mg; Potassium: 70mg

Difficulty Rating: ☆

Tips: Add a sprinkle of paprika for extra flavor.

160. Rice Cake with Avocado and Tomato

Servings: 1
Preparation time: 5 minutes
Ingredients:

- 1 rice cake
- 1/4 avocado, mashed
- 1 small tomato, sliced

Directions:

1. Spread the mashed avocado onto the rice cake.
2. Top with sliced tomato.

Nutritional Values per Serving: Calories: 63 kcal; Protein: 2.25 g; Carbohydrates: 15g; Dietary Fiber: 3g; Total Fat: 5g; Saturated Fat: 1g; Cholesterol: 0mg; Sodium: 10mg; Phosphorus: 80mg; Potassium: 200mg

Difficulty Rating: ☆

Tips: Sprinkle with a pinch of sea salt for added flavor.

161. Easy Berry Parfait

Servings: 4
Preparation time: 10 minutes
Cooking time: None
Ingredients:
- 2 cups of mixed berries (strawberries, blueberries, raspberries)
- 1 cup of plain Greek yogurt
- 2 tablespoons of sugar-free granola

Directions:
1. Wash and slice the berries.
2. In a glass or bowl, layer the berries and yogurt.
3. Repeat the layers until all the ingredients are used.
4. Top with sugar-free granola.

Nutritional Values per Serving: 473 kcal; Protein: 47 g; Carbohydrates: 18g; Dietary Fiber: 4g; Total Fat: 2g; Saturated Fat: 0g; Cholesterol: 0mg; Sodium: 20mg; Phosphorus: 80mg; Potassium: 200mg

Difficulty Rating: ☆ ☆
Tips: Use different types of berries or add a sprinkle of cinnamon for extra flavor.
Average cost: $3

162. Chocolate Avocado Mousse

Servings: 2
Preparation time: 15 minutes
Cooking time: None
Ingredients:
- 1 ripe avocado
- 2 tablespoons of unsweetened cocoa powder
- 2 tablespoons of sugar-free sweetener
- 1/2 teaspoon of vanilla extract
- 1/4 cup of unsweetened almond milk

Directions:
1. Scoop out the flesh of the avocado and place it in a blender or food processor.
2. Add the cocoa powder, sweetener, vanilla extract, and almond milk.
3. Blend until smooth and creamy.
4. Divide the mousse into serving dishes and refrigerate for at least 1 hour before serving.

Nutritional Values per Serving: Calories: 359 kcal; Protein: 7 g; Carbohydrates: 9g; Dietary Fiber: 6g; Total Fat: 15g; Saturated Fat: 2g; Cholesterol: 0mg; Sodium: 10mg; Phosphorus: 100mg; Potassium: 400mg

Difficulty Rating: ☆ ☆ ☆
Tips: Add a pinch of cinnamon or a sprinkle of chopped nuts on top for added crunch.
Average cost: $2.50

163. Apple Cinnamon Oatmeal Cookies

Servings: 12
Preparation time: 15 minutes
Cooking time: 15 minutes
Ingredients:
- 1 cup of rolled oats
- 1 cup of almond flour
- 1/4 cup of sugar-free sweetener
- 1 teaspoon of ground cinnamon
- 1/2 teaspoon of baking powder
- 1/4 teaspoon of salt
- 1/4 cup of unsweetened applesauce
- 2 tablespoons of melted coconut oil
- 1/2 teaspoon of vanilla extract

Directions:
1. Preheat the oven to 350°F (175°C), and line a baking sheet with parchment paper.
2. In a large bowl, combine the oats, almond flour, sweetener, cinnamon, baking powder, and salt.
3. In a separate bowl, whisk together the applesauce, coconut oil, and vanilla extract.
4. Add the wet ingredients to the dry ingredients and mix until well combined.
5. Drop spoonfuls of the dough onto the prepared baking sheet and flatten them with the back of a spoon.
6. Bake for 15 minutes or until golden brown.

Nutritional Values per Serving: Calories: 4146 kcal; Protein: 138 g; Carbohydrates: 8g; Dietary Fiber: 2g; Total Fat: 6g; Saturated Fat: 3g; Cholesterol: 0mg; Sodium: 60mg; Phosphorus: 50mg; Potassium: 100mg

Difficulty Rating: ☆☆☆
Tips: Add raisins or chopped nuts to the dough for extra texture.
Average cost: $3.50

164. Banana Ice Cream

Servings: 2
Preparation time: 5 minutes
Cooking time: None
Ingredients:
- 2 ripe bananas, sliced and frozen
- 2 tablespoons of unsweetened almond milk
- 1/2 teaspoon of vanilla extract

Directions:
1. Place the frozen banana slices, almond milk, and vanilla extract in a blender or food processor.
2. Blend until smooth and creamy, scraping down the sides as needed.
3. Serve immediately as soft-serve ice cream or transfer to a container and freeze for a firmer texture.

Nutritional Values per Serving: Calories: 434 kcal; Protein: 6.2 g; Carbohydrates: 30g; Dietary Fiber: 3g; Total Fat: 0g; Saturated Fat: 0g; Cholesterol: 0mg; Sodium: 0mg; Phosphorus: 40mg; Potassium: 400mg

Difficulty Rating: ☆
Tips: Add a tablespoon of unsweetened cocoa powder for a chocolatey twist.
Average cost: $1.50

165. Lemon Chia Seed Pudding

Servings: 4
Preparation time: 10 minutes
Cooking time: None
Ingredients:
- 1 cup of unsweetened almond milk
- 1/4 cup of chia seeds
- 2 tablespoons of sugar-free sweetener
- Zest and juice of 1 lemon

Directions:
1. In a bowl, whisk together the almond milk, chia seeds, sweetener, lemon zest, and lemon juice.
2. Let the mixture sit for 5 minutes, then whisk again to prevent clumping.
3. Cover the bowl and refrigerate for at least 2 hours or overnight.
4. Stir well before serving and divide into individual servings.

Nutritional Values per Serving: Calories: 318 kcal; Protein: 18 g; Carbohydrates: 8g; Dietary Fiber: 6g; Total Fat: 4g; Saturated Fat: 0g; Cholesterol: 0mg; Sodium: 20mg; Phosphorus: 100mg; Potassium: 100mg

Difficulty Rating: ☆ ☆

Tips: Add a teaspoon of vanilla extract or top with fresh berries for extra flavor.

Average cost: $2.50

166. Peanut Butter Energy Balls

Servings: 10
Preparation time: 10 minutes
Cooking time: None
Ingredients:
- 1 cup of rolled oats
- 1/2 cup of natural peanut butter
- 1/4 cup of sugar-free sweetener
- 2 tablespoons of ground flaxseed
- 2 tablespoons of unsweetened cocoa powder
- 1/4 cup of unsweetened almond milk

Directions:
1. In a large bowl, combine the oats, peanut butter, sweetener, flaxseed, cocoa powder, and almond milk.
2. Mix until well combined and the mixture holds together.
3. Roll the mixture into small balls, about 1 inch in diameter.
4. Place the energy balls on a baking sheet lined with parchment paper and refrigerate for at least 30 minutes before serving.

Nutritional Values per Serving: Calories: 2676 kcal; Protein: 120 g; Carbohydrates: 12g; Dietary Fiber: 4g; Total Fat: 8g; Saturated Fat: 1g; Cholesterol: 0mg; Sodium: 40mg; Phosphorus: 80mg; Potassium: 150mg

Difficulty Rating: ☆ ☆

Tips: Add chopped nuts or dried fruits for added texture and flavor.

Average cost: $3

167. Vanilla Chia Pudding

Servings: 4
Preparation time: 5 minutes
Cooking time: None
Ingredients:
- 1 cup of unsweetened almond milk
- 1/4 cup of chia seeds
- 2 tablespoons of sugar-free sweetener
- 1/2 teaspoon of vanilla extract

Directions:
1. In a bowl, whisk together the almond milk, chia seeds, sweetener, and vanilla extract.
2. Let the mixture sit for 5 minutes, then whisk again to prevent clumping.
3. Cover the bowl and refrigerate for at least 2 hours or overnight.
4. Stir well before serving and divide into individual servings.

Nutritional Values per Serving: Calories: 318 kcal; Protein: 18 g; Carbohydrates: 8g; Dietary Fiber: 6g; Total Fat: 4g; Saturated Fat: 0g; Cholesterol: 0mg; Sodium: 20mg; Phosphorus: 100mg; Potassium: 100mg

Difficulty Rating: ☆

Tips: Add a sprinkle of cinnamon or top with fresh fruit for extra flavor.

Average cost: $2.50

168. Baked Cinnamon Apple Chips

Servings: 4
Preparation time: 10 minutes
Cooking time: 2 hours
Ingredients:
- 2 apples, cored and thinly sliced
- 1 teaspoon of ground cinnamon
- 1/2 teaspoon of sugar-free sweetener

Directions:
1. Preheat the oven to 200°F (95°C) and line a baking sheet with parchment paper.
2. In a bowl, toss the apple slices with cinnamon and sweetener until coated.
3. Arrange the apple slices in a single layer on the prepared baking sheet.
4. Bake for 2 hours or until the chips are crisp, flipping them halfway through.

Nutritional Values per Serving: Calories: 418 kcal; Protein: 2.4 g; Carbohydrates: 15g; Dietary Fiber: 4g; Total Fat: 0g; Saturated Fat: 0g; Cholesterol: 0mg; Sodium: 0mg; Phosphorus: 20mg; Potassium: 100mg

Difficulty Rating: ☆ ☆

Tips: Sprinkle with a pinch of nutmeg or drizzle with melted dark chocolate for a treat.

Average cost: $2

169. Pumpkin Spice Muffins

Servings: 12
Preparation time: 15 minutes
Cooking time: 20 minutes
Ingredients:
- 1 cup of almond flour
- 1/2 cup of coconut flour
- 1/4 cup of sugar-free sweetener
- 1 teaspoon of baking powder
- 1/2 teaspoon of baking soda
- 1/2 teaspoon of ground cinnamon
- 1/4 teaspoon of ground nutmeg
- 1/4 teaspoon of ground ginger
- 1/4 teaspoon of salt
- 1 cup of canned pumpkin puree
- 1/4 cup of unsweetened almond milk
- 2 tablespoons of melted coconut oil
- 2 large eggs

Directions:
1. Preheat the oven to 350°F (175°C) and line a muffin tin with paper liners.
2. In a large bowl, whisk together the almond flour, coconut flour, sweetener, baking powder, baking soda, cinnamon, nutmeg, ginger, and salt.
3. In a separate bowl, whisk together the pumpkin puree, almond milk, coconut oil, and eggs.
4. Add the wet ingredients to the dry ingredients and mix until just combined.
5. Divide the batter evenly among the muffin cups.
6. Bake for 20 minutes or until a toothpick inserted into the center comes out clean.

Nutritional Values per Serving: 449 kcal; Protein: 156 g; Carbohydrates: 8g; Dietary Fiber: 4g; Total Fat: 10g; Saturated Fat: 5g; Cholesterol: 35mg; Sodium: 180mg; Phosphorus: 100mg; Potassium: 150mg

Difficulty Rating: ☆☆☆
Tips: Add chopped walnuts or raisins to the batter for added texture and flavor.
Average cost: $4

170. Greek Yogurt Bark

Servings: 8
Preparation time: 10 minutes
Cooking time: 2 hours
Ingredients:
- 2 cups of plain Greek yogurt
- 2 tablespoons of sugar-free sweetener
- 1/2 teaspoon of vanilla extract
- 1/4 cup of unsweetened shredded coconut
- 1/4 cup of chopped nuts (almonds, walnuts, or pistachios)
- 1/4 cup of sugar-free dark chocolate chips

Directions:
1. In a bowl, mix together the Greek yogurt, sweetener, and vanilla extract.
2. Line a baking sheet with parchment paper and spread the yogurt mixture evenly.
3. Sprinkle the shredded coconut, chopped nuts, and dark chocolate chips over the yogurt.
4. Freeze for at least 2 hours or until firm.
5. Break the bark into pieces and serve immediately.

Nutritional Values per Serving: 364 kcal; Protein: 200 g; Carbohydrates: 6g; Dietary Fiber: 2g; Total Fat: 8g; Saturated Fat: 4g; Cholesterol: 0mg; Sodium: 20mg; Phosphorus: 80mg; Potassium: 200mg

Difficulty Rating: ☆☆
Tips: Add dried fruit or a sprinkle of cinnamon for extra flavor and texture.
Average cost: $3.50

CHAPTER 19: CONVERSION CHART

Volume Equivalents (Liquid)

US Standard	US Standard (ounces)	Metric (approximate)
2 tablespoons	1 fl. oz.	30 mL
¼ cup	2 fl. oz.	60 mL
½ cup	4 fl. oz.	120 mL
1 cup	8 fl. oz.	240 mL
1½ cups	12 fl. oz.	355 mL
2 cups or 1 pint	16 fl. oz.	475 mL
4 cups or 1 quart	32 fl. oz.	1 L
1 gallon	128 fl. oz.	4 L

Volume Equivalents (Dry)

US Standard	Metric (approximate)
⅛ teaspoon	0.5 mL
¼ teaspoon	1 mL
½ teaspoon	2 mL
¾ teaspoon	4 mL
1 teaspoon	5 mL

1 tablespoon	15 mL
¼ cup	59 mL
⅓ cup	79 mL
½ cup	118 mL
⅔ cup	156 mL
¾ cup	177 mL
1 cup	235 mL
2 cups or 1 pint	475 mL
3 cups	700 mL
4 cups or 1 quart	1 L

Oven Temperatures

Fahrenheit (F)	Celsius (C) (approximate)
250 deg. F	120°C
300 deg. F	150°C
325 deg. F	165°C
350 deg. F	180°C
375 deg. F	190°C
400 deg. F	200°C

425 deg. F	220°C
450 deg. F	230°C

Weight Equivalents

US Standard	Metric (approximate)
1 tablespoon	15 g
½ ounce	15 g
1 ounce	30 g
2 ounces	60 g
4 ounces	115 g
8 ounces	225 g
12 ounces	340 g
16 ounces or 1 pound	455 g

INDEX

Almond Flour Blueberry Muffins; 127
Apple and Almond Butter Slices; 120
Apple Cinnamon Crumble; 98
Apple Cinnamon Energy Bites; 93
Apple Cinnamon Mug Cake; 124
Apple Cinnamon Oatmeal Cookies; 149
Apple Slices with Peanut Butter; 145
Avocado and Tomato Salad; 118
Avocado and Tomato Toast; 107
Avocado Hummus; 94
Avocado Toast; 69; 80
Avocado Toast with Egg; 130
Baked Chicken Parmesan; 91
Baked Cinnamon Apple Chips; 151
Baked Cod with Lemon and Herbs; 92
Baked Peaches with Honey and Cinnamon; 101
Baked Salmon with Dill Sauce; 138
Baked Salmon with Roasted Vegetables:; 88
Baked Sweet Potato Chips; 144
Baked Sweet Potato Fries; 96
Banana Ice Cream; 149
Banana Oatmeal Cookies; 99
Beef and Broccoli Stir-Fry; 114
Berry and Spinach Smoothie; 106
Berry Chia Pudding; 97
Berry Smoothie; 70; 122
Berry Smoothie Bowl; 82
Black Bean and Corn Salad; 117
Black Bean and Vegetable Quesadilla; 136
Breakfast Burrito; 131
Caprese Pasta Salad; 75; 109
Caprese Salad; 87
Caprese Skewers; 120
Caprese Stuffed Chicken Breast; 116
Chia Pudding with Berries; 124
Chicken and Vegetable Stir-Fry; 83; 133
Chickpea and Vegetable Stir-Fry; 75
Chickpea Salad; 93
Chocolate Avocado Mousse; 98; 148
Chocolate Banana Pudding; 123
Cottage Cheese and Berries; 146
Cottage Cheese and Fruit Bowl; 131
Cottage Cheese and Fruit Salad; 82
Cucumber and Cream Cheese Bites; 121
Cucumber Mint Water; 97
Easy Berry Parfait; 148
Edamame Salad; 121
Egg and Vegetable Muffin Cups; 72
Egg Salad Lettuce Wraps; 111
Eggplant Parmesan; 142
Fruit and Nut Breakfast Quinoa; 107
Fruit and Yogurt Smoothie; 132
Greek Chicken Pita; 110
Greek Salad with Grilled Chicken; 86; 136; 142
Greek Yogurt and Berry Parfait; 76
Greek Yogurt Bark; 152
Greek Yogurt Parfait; 69; 78; 103; 129; 143
Greek Yogurt with Berries; 118
Greek Yogurt with Honey and Walnuts; 125
Grilled Chicken Caesar Salad; 68; 108
Grilled Chicken Salad; 73
Grilled Chicken with Balsamic Glaze; 113
Grilled Lemon Herb Chicken; 88
Grilled Lemon Herb Chicken Breast; 138
Grilled Salmon with Lemon and Dill; 113
Hard-Boiled Eggs with Salt and Pepper; 147
Lemon Chia Seed Pudding; 150
Lemon Yogurt Parfait; 99
Lentil and Vegetable Soup; 91; 134; 141
Lentil Soup; 85
Mango Coconut Chia Popsicles; 126
Mediterranean Tuna Salad; 115
Mini Caprese Skewers; 146
Oatmeal Raisin Energy Balls; 102
Oatmeal with Berries and Nuts; 128
Overnight Chia Pudding; 71; 79; 104
Peanut Butter Banana Ice Cream; 100
Peanut Butter Banana Wrap; 71
Peanut Butter Energy Balls; 125; 150
Pumpkin Spice Muffins; 152
Quinoa and Black Bean Salad; 139
Quinoa and Vegetable Salad; 135
Quinoa and Vegetable Stir-Fry; 108
Quinoa Breakfast Bowl; 72; 80
Quinoa Fruit Salad; 100
Quinoa Salad; 83
Quinoa Salad Cups; 95
Quinoa Salad with Roasted Vegetables; 116
Quinoa Stuffed Bell Peppers; 73
Quinoa Stuffed Bell Peppers:; 89
Raspberry Chia Jam; 126
Rice Cake with Avocado and Tomato; 147
Roasted Chickpeas; 122; 143
Salmon and Asparagus Foil Pack; 85; 110

Salmon and Asparagus Foil Packets; 137
Scrambled Egg and Avocado Wrap; 103
Scrambled Egg and Vegetable Wrap; 78
Scrambled Eggs with Vegetables; 128
Shrimp and Broccoli Stir-Fry; 90; 141
Shrimp Stir-Fry with Vegetables; 77; 114
Smoked Salmon and Cream Cheese Bagel; 106
Spinach and Feta Omelette; 68; 74; 104
Spinach and Feta Quiche Cups; 81
Spinach and Feta Stuffed Chicken Breast; 140
Spinach and Mushroom Frittata; 117
Spinach and Mushroom Omelette; 84; 135
Strawberry Banana Smoothie; 102
Strawberry Yogurt Parfait; 123
Tofu and Vegetable Stir-Fry; 87
Tuna and Avocado Wrap; 74
Tuna and White Bean Salad; 112
Tuna Lettuce Wraps; 96
Tuna Salad Lettuce Wraps; 119; 134; 145
Turkey and Avocado Wrap; 109; 133
Turkey and Hummus Wrap; 76
Turkey and Vegetable Stir-Fry; 139
Turkey and Vegetable Stir-Fry:; 89
Turkey Lettuce Wraps; 84
Vanilla Chia Pudding; 151
Vanilla Chia Seed Pudding; 101
Vegetable and Chickpea Curry; 92
Vegetable Curry with Brown Rice; 140
Vegetable Omelette; 79; 130
Veggie and Cheese Breakfast Quesadilla; 105
Veggie and Hummus Wrap; 86; 111; 137
Veggie and Tofu Curry; 90
Veggie Breakfast Burrito; 70; 81
Veggie Breakfast Wrap; 132
Veggie Omelette; 112; 115
Veggie Pita Pocket; 77
Veggie Sticks with Hummus; 144
Veggie Stuffed Mini Peppers; 94
Veggie Wrap; 119
Watermelon Fruit Pizza; 127
Whole Wheat Banana Pancakes; 105
Whole Wheat Pancakes; 129
Zucchini Chips; 95

Made in the USA
Las Vegas, NV
09 April 2024